Love Has Many Faces

BY

LISA MORGAN

With Nuala Giblin

ISBN: 978-1-5262-0256-7

Contents

Acknowledgements

Lisa Morgan was a British national, working in the Middle East, when she met Boaz, the love of her life and moved to Uganda to start a new life. Within months the dream had turned into a nightmare after she was left penniless, heartbroken and fighting for her life in a foreign land. This is the story, in her own words, of Lisa's fight for justice, how she survived the ultimate betrayal, tragedy and escaped to tell the tale.

Kindness and help comes from the heart, not just from the pocket

Prologue

"He's not coming."

"Excuse me?"

"He would have been here by now if he was."

The taxi driver had a point. I had been waiting at Entebbe airport for nearly one hour. After coming through passport control, I grabbed my bags off the carousel and headed for the exit. I ended up standing by the taxi rank. People were coming and going but despite the hustle and bustle, all I could hear was this tinny 60's music, coming from inside. I'd been standing there so long I'd heard the same songs over and over again. I kept looking at my watch and then looking around but there was no sign of him. I couldn't ring him as I'd left my mobile behind in Lebanon. I'd been horrified when I realised it was still on the charger. Luckily my friend Rita and her sister Maria had come to wave me off at the airport. I'd been using Rita's SIM card which had all my contacts so I wrote his number on the inside of my plane ticket. I had left Lebanon on such a high. It was my birthday and the girls had made such a fuss. They even surprised me with a '*Happy Birthday*' cushion.

I was coming to Uganda to start a new life with Boaz. I had never been to Africa before but I was so excited. After all, this was the biggest decision I had ever made; my very own big adventure. But the excitement was beginning to turn to doubt. Where was he? Maybe he's caught up in traffic or got delayed while looking at apartments? I had been expecting to see him in the lovely brown, pin-striped shirt that I'd bought. I liked to spoil Boaz and last Christmas I bought him a very expensive Omega watch from the UK. I hadn't given it to him yet as it was a surprise wedding gift. I hope he likes it. I was forever finding excuses to buy him clothes. But this shirt was special. I had found it in a small shop in Texas; having spotted it on a mannequin in a shop window. The shop was about to close but I banged on the door until the shopkeeper let me in. I knew the shirt would look beautiful against his dark skin. We had agreed he would wear it to make it easier for me to pick him out from the crowds. But he was nowhere to be seen. And as everyone has mobiles nowadays, I couldn't see a single phone box either.

"I will be back in 20 minutes and if you are still here I will take you somewhere," said the taxi driver as he drove off. But where? I had no idea where I was or where I was going. Twenty minutes later he was back. I was feeling a bit embarrassed and decided to let him help me.

"What is the number of this guy?" asked the taxi driver. I was still unsure of his motive but I read out the number. He rang the number but no answer. I was now starting to panic and my mouth was dry. Earlier, while changing planes in Ethiopia, I went to use the bathroom. I very cheekily asked the cleaner if I could use her phone to make a missed call to Boaz. I couldn't leave a message as Boaz didn't have voicemail but once he spotted the missed call, he'd call back. Wouldn't he? I had an hour and a half to kill before my connecting flight so I sat near the cleaner just in case. But the phone never rang. Admittedly there had been times when I would call Boaz from Lebanon and he wouldn't answer. He would claim that the signal wasn't good wherever he was. My experience of third world countries and a bad signal wasn't unusual, so I had no reason not to believe him.

By now the heat was overwhelming and panic was beginning to set in. Now this is someone who is never late. We had met while working in Iraq and he was always on time. In fact, he was usually early. Oh, my god. What if something has happened to him?

"There isn't another airport is there?" I asked feebly. I was determined not to burst into tears in front of this stranger.
"No this is the only one. I will try the number again." I could see in his eyes that he felt sorry for me.

This time Boaz answered. The taxi driver handed me the phone. Now I was annoyed. I had crossed a continent to be with this man. "Where are

you? I'm at the airport."
"Sorry sorry, traffic. I am on my way."

He sounded surprised to hear my voice. I didn't want to have this conversation on somebody else's phone so I simply asked how long he would be.

"Not long. About 20 minutes."

When Boaz finally turned up, he looked pleased to see me and gave me a big hug but something wasn't right. I couldn't put my finger on it. I admit I didn't have much of a smile on my face, and the excitement had long gone. But then this was not the welcome I was expecting.

"Let's take a picture of you at the airport. Like a tourist."
"Really?"

The last thing I wanted was to have my picture taken. I'd only just got off a plane for God's sake. All I wanted was to know where we would be living and what plans he had for our future. But one thing I knew for certain was that something or someone had changed. Could it be that I was about to make the biggest mistake of my life?

Chapter One

My Big Fat Adventure

"Okay, let's go. Do you have everything Morgan?" asked Rita.
"Yeah I'm ready, let's do this." Rita and Maria were driving me to Beirut Airport. This was my last day in Lebanon and I'm going to miss the place. I took my last breath of the Lebanese sea air as I stood on the balcony looking over to the Mediterranean Sea.

"Come on, get in the car," said Rita.
"Okay, okay I'm coming."
"We're going to be late."
"Not the way you drive you 'crazy' woman," I laughed. We all started laughing especially when Rita's parents tripped over my baggage to say goodbye.

It was a very exciting day for me. Not only was it my birthday but I was on my way to Africa to start my new life with Boaz, my very lovely Ugandan boyfriend, soon to be husband.

Lebanon had been my vacation home for the last seven years while working as a security contractor in Iraq. The commute is a lot less than going all the way back to the UK. One hour and twenty minutes from Baghdad Airport to Beirut. Then slip into a bikini and slide down a very cold beer; beautiful. You can't fail to have a good time in Lebanon. The beaches, the mountains, the food; I love it all. It's taken one very special person to drag me away from here.

Rita was a secretary for a lady I'd had an interview with. I was trying to get into the Lebanese job market for when the Iraqi war came to an end. I didn't get the job but I did gain a very good friend, with a wicked sense of humour. Maria was the middle sister to Rita. She was totally free-spirited and lived life for the moment. To be honest you couldn't wish for better friends; they were like my sisters. I got on well with all the family and her Mum even said she'd love to adopt me! I think she was joking but I did wonder how I'd explain to her friends that her adopted daughter was about the same age as her.

It's funny how you change your mind when you see life through different eyes.

When I was very young my mother used to tell me that my bedroom looked like Beirut. I never understood what she meant but always smiled, thinking she was saying something nice. In the late 70's and 80's I'd heard my Mum and Dad talk a lot about Beirut.

I only ever got to see the troubles on a black and white TV set through the crack of the door, and then my Mum would 'shoo' me to bed. She wanted to keep these 12-year-old eyes and ears innocent.

I later understood my mum was referring to my bedroom as a bombsite. Well that was my Mum; she always saw the humour in both positive and negative situations. Funny how life works outs though. She was almost responsible for my curiosity about the Middle East and why I wanted to understand what these people were fighting about. Sad thing is she never knew I pursued a career in security, training as a Close Protection Officer, with a Diploma in Special Weapons and Tactics. I worked for some of the largest blue chip companies in London before heading to the Middle East.

I first visited Beirut in 2005 when Sam, a Lebanese pilot who brought passengers from Beirut to Baghdad Airport, where I worked, suggested that I would love Lebanon and should visit one day. I was a bit apprehensive about going from one warzone to another, just for a vacation. So one Saturday afternoon I was sat on Jo's settee. It was a dreary day in Grimsby and we were watching an old black and white movie and bored to death, when suddenly I had this idea.

"Come on, we're going into town."
"Great," Jo replied, "what pub are we going in?"
"No, we're going to the travel agents; I want to buy myself a ticket to Beirut."
"Do what?"

A new adventure was born. I threw Trip Advisor's advice to the wind and booked my ticket. Beirut, here I come.

I'd been a contractor in Iraq since 2004, eight months after the invasion in 2003. After a while it weighs heavy on your mind. The things you see; the things you hear. It's almost like a madness and you start asking yourself is all this worth it? Wars have been going on for thousands of years and there's still no end in sight. Welcome to mankind.

I sometimes feel guilty that I was a small part of that war. The only good thing I can say about my involvement is I was never there to harm anybody, to fight against anybody. I held a very responsible position that came with much danger, not just to me but my colleagues too.

I lost a dear friend in a suicide attack at one of our checkpoints. A car refused to stop and all weapons were drawn. There was lots of shouting in different languages; a lot of confusion. When the car came to a halt and the dust settled, everything changed at the flick of a switch.

I was responsible for the security training at Baghdad's International Airport and it was hard for me not to be sympathetic or care about the Iraqi people. They were equally confused about what was going on. Their futures were hanging in the balance.

These workers took a massive risk; to work for a foreign company or for the US military meant they were seen as traitors. Plus, they had to make the journey from Baghdad using route Irish; the most dangerous and notorious road on the planet. It is like a 12 kilometre obstacle course littered with sniper fire, roadside attacks; the dangers are endless. Then they had to make that journey all the way back again. Plus, there was the constant fear of their families being threatened, injured or killed, while going about their daily lives. It's hideous to think how many lives have been lost just to capture one man, Saddam Hussein. I'm not even convinced he was that terrible; as dictatorships go. I am sure most will agree Iraq was probably better when he was in power. Ten years on I can only pray for the Iraqi people and their safety.

Now, as we headed for Beirut airport, I can honestly say I was looking forward to a rest on the plane. I had been up all night with Rita and her sisters. It was like a proper sleepover, although nobody actually slept. Rita had been asking me leading questions about African men. The Lebanese ladies have certain restrictions regarding what you can and can't do, especially before marriage. So she would take advantage of my British, liberal ways. I would normally change the subject or run away to the bathroom so I didn't have to answer. I'm actually quite conservative and shy when it comes to talking about sex.

But it was my last night. As we settled down to sleep I heard, "So Morgan, is it true what they say about black men?" I didn't know what to say so I pretended I was asleep. There was a brief silence. "Morgan, don't pretend you're asleep." Dammit, I can't get out of this.

"Well, put it this way, you don't know if you are making love or pole dancing."

All the girls burst out laughing. Isn't laughing one of the best feelings ever?

We arrived at the airport, parked the car and headed for the check-in desk.

"Back in a minute," said Rita, "I just need to go the shop." Maria went with her as I sorted out my bags and passport.

"Happy Birthday to you. Happy Birthday to you."

I turned around and the girls surprised me with a pink, fluffy 'Happy Birthday' cushion. How lovely. I couldn't have wished for a better send off.

"Okay Morgan," said Rita. The girls always called me Morgan. "Check you've got everything, passport, phone."
Phone where is my phone? I started to panic. I could visualise my phone. I had left it on the charger at Rita's house.
"What am I going to do? I can't go back for it, there isn't time."
"Don't worry Morgan, I have all your numbers here," said Rita.

Thank God. I had been using Rita's spare SIM card, as I had cancelled my Lebanese phone contract. All I needed was Boaz's number. I wrote it down on the inside of my ticket; that way I wouldn't lose it. I also wrote down Rita's number. She wanted me to call her when I got there.

"Okay, better go now. I will call you. Miss you already. Love you."

Once I boarded the plane I got myself settled. I was well on my way. All I could think about was my future and my new life with Boaz. I started thinking about the strong connection we had; the common interests and the similarities between him and my brother. It was a massive loss for me when my brother took his own life. I was very lonely for many years afterwards. And when Boaz told me about his time in the military it drew me closer to him. Like my brother, Boaz had been posted to the Congo and could also speak Swahili. Boaz could also speak the Pygmy language and my brother used to tell me stories about the Pygmies. Boaz had lost someone too. His father was in the Ugandan Army and had died of his injuries after being shot.

It was obvious to me that Boaz and I found comfort in each other. We had both suffered losses and were like two lost souls destined to be with each other.

All I knew was for the very first time in my life I actually felt a connection, a bond with somebody. I could really relate to this person. And I trusted Boaz enough to leave my job and move to his country to be with him. Boaz was my Mr Right and meant everything to me. After working in the war torn Middle East I finally had the chance of love and happiness. It might be on another continent but love is where the heart is and my heart was waiting for me in Uganda.

Boaz and I were friends at first. I never saw him as a boyfriend. He was Ugandan and a real charmer. He worked in Operations and was in his early 30's. All the other Ugandans looked up to him and called him Mzee, which is Ugandan for elder. He was probably the oldest amongst them and the most experienced. Boaz was very handsome and very likable and

15

popular especially with the ex-pats. He was the one the bosses turned to when they needed someone to organise any events. Boaz got on with everyone. We'd go running together and to the gym but I never looked at him as anything but a friend.

But I was beginning to miss him when he wasn't around.

The Ugandans could only go home every two years as visas were hard to get. So Boaz was really excited about his trip home. He had all these plans for his future; land, cattle and a house of his own. I so admired him. He didn't have the easiest of starts in life. He came from a remote village near Ibanda about four hours from Kampala. His mother died not long after he was born so his grandmother brought him up. Her husband was also married to her sister. But as I later found out – *TIA - 'This Is Africa.'*

We had so much in common but not only the military connection. I was adopted and both my adoptive parents are now dead along with my brother. My biological mother didn't want anything to do with me. So we were both orphans.

Boaz was flying home and had asked me to come and sit with him at the airport while he waited. I wanted to buy him a small gift so I ran to the airport shop. I bought a nice Pears soap in a box and put $50 US dollars inside. I wrote a little note – *Enjoy your vacation. I want to hear all about how you spent the $50* - and put that inside the box as well. He was under strict instructions not to open it until he got on the plane. He called me from Dubai and again when he reached Uganda, saying thank you and how much he was missing me. I thought it was a little strange and wasn't quite sure what to say.

I didn't see Boaz again for two months as I was in Lebanon when he got back. On my return the first thing I did was go to the Ops room to say hello. I had missed him too. I sat with him for hours. He was so easy to talk to.

The friendship began to grow deeper. Boaz was such a gentleman. He would carry my bags to my trailer when I arrived back from vacation. I remember he had the loveliest, warmest hands and he made me feel like

I was sixteen again. I couldn't stop thinking about him. I realised there was a lot more to him than met the eye. He was quite deep and would write love notes, slip them into my bag or under the door.

Boaz would walk me back to my trailer and ask if he could come in but I always said no. But I couldn't close the door in his face, as I was a smoker and kept the door open. So it wasn't easy. It was over a year before I let him in. He stood by the wall but wouldn't come near me. It was a strange moment. Am I going to be the one to seduce this young man? I could feel this urgent sexual attraction between us. Should I just start kissing him? Maybe if I do it badly it will scare him off and that would be the end of that. So I did but the kiss felt amazing. I didn't want it to end and neither did he. But now I was in trouble. How was I going to get him out of my trailer without anyone seeing?

Our relationship had to be kept a secret. Liaisons between staff were not encouraged. Plus, a relationship between an ex-pat and a humble Ugandan was a definite no no. We would go out jogging and share a little kiss but we had to be so careful. Whenever he passed my trailer he'd knock and I would knock back. Very childish, but quite lovely too. He'd buy me phone cards and wouldn't take any money; collect my laundry bag, write me love notes. Even rush to get me a chair to sit on so I could watch him play football. He didn't seem to care if anyone saw; Boaz wore his heart on his sleeve. Simple things but these small things meant more to me than anything money could buy.

We would meet for coffee and if I worked a night shift he'd come to the airport to see me. I really wanted to hold his hand and show him off as my boyfriend but I couldn't. Boaz had requested I bring a picture back from my vacation. So now he had a framed picture of me in his trailer but he had to hide it on top of his wardrobe, but it could still be seen. And someone did see it and asked why he had a picture of Lisa? Boaz replied, "She is beautiful and I'm going to marry her," and laughed like it was a joke.

Boaz was attractive with lovely white teeth. Boy was I jealous of those teeth. He was small framed with not an ounce of fat and very athletic. He was an exceptionally good runner and very good at football. The secrecy heightened the relationship and made it more romantic. And Boaz was such good company. He was smart and a voracious reader.

He was easy going and always well turned out. I remembered what my brother used to say. "You can tell a lot about a man by his shoes," and Boaz's shoes were always highly polished.

We had been together for nearly a year when he asked me to marry him. It was 6th August 2011. I didn't see the proposal coming. We were sat on my step chatting. And it seemed the most natural thing in the world to say yes. He was my soulmate and I knew I wanted to spend the rest of my life with him and he was such a responsible person. You knew he would be happy to see you happy. And whenever we were together it felt lovely, like that nice, warm glow after your first glass of wine.

Boaz's name had always fascinated me. I had never met a Boaz before. Now I was marrying a Boaz I wanted to know more. It was my friend Randy who explained a bit more about the name. I'd been chatting with him about my future plans with Boaz.

He asked me if I knew the biblical story of Boaz from Bethlehem; I didn't. But I'm sure I was about to hear it. Randy is very religious and had been brought up around the Bible Belt of America. I sometimes wonder how we ever became friends, being the unbeliever that I am. But he was a good soul and that was all that mattered.

I can't say that I'm very religious nor do I claim to be an atheist but I do think that perhaps a scientific view rather than an old tale has slightly more depth. Anyway, I normally put those types of conversations into my, 'not very interested categories' – right next to spoon bending.
Randy began to tell me that Boaz was a rich landowner from Bethlehem; a generous man. Now Ruth was a poor widow and they met while she was gleaning grain in his fields. The story is from *The Book of Ruth* and focuses on the love and kindness Boaz extended to this poor widow, Ruth. They go on to marry, have children and Ruth is the great grandmother of King David; the one who defeated Goliath.

Randy told me that the love between Boaz and Ruth is an example of just one of the many wonderful principles of today's life. And how it is God's love that helps those who have endured tragic situations. "Yeah," I replied trying to show some interest.

Randy continued on, "Ruth was a poor widow and a foreigner, yet God used her as part of the family line leading to Jesus." Then he really got into his stride. "Genuine love and kindness will be rewarded. God abundantly blesses those who seek obedient lives. Obedient living does not allow for accidents in God's plan. God's sovereign power can be 'seen'. He is in control of just about everything that happens, even when we do not understand the situation."

Oh sweet Jesus I thought and looked up, hoping he'd finished.

"Well, yes, okay that's very interesting." I paused. "So if God is in control of everything, he might want to explain why he let me crash my brother's car into a parked vehicle. My Mum wasn't very understanding and it cost me two weeks' salary."

"Lisa don't you take anything seriously?"

I just smiled and then we both laughed.

Joking aside I did think about what he'd said and for the next few weeks it got me thinking. I'm quite the law-abiding citizen. I've never had a speeding ticket, well never got caught, put it that way or even been inside a Police station. Maybe that represents 'obedient living.' Who knows? And could Boaz and I have crossed paths because we had both endured tragic situations? Losing our parents at such an early age. Maybe I'm about to be saved? To me Boaz really was my knight in shining armour. I had never felt happier with anyone before in my life. Boaz was the missing jigsaw piece.

I admit I was captivated by the whole story of Boaz. It's funny how someone's name can have such an impact on you. Well either way I found Boaz totally enchanting. And now I was going to be Mrs Boaz.

Chapter Two

TIA – This is Africa

I had this idea that as Uganda is a developing country; it would be easier to start up a business there. Especially if you already had the capital needed. The UK has become so expensive and I had got used to waking up to sunshine every day. Boaz was sure I'd love his country as much as he did. He was full of ideas which I loved. He was fixed on a moneylending business which can be quite rewarding with a good return. He wanted to buy some cattle and a piece of land and build a house. I was set on buying land and starting up my own small construction company building houses. It really was an exciting time.

By now I was in my 40s and knew that a young man like Boaz, who was twelve years younger than me, would want a family. Before starting my new adventure to Uganda I visited Randy and his wife Cathee in Texas. They were delighted by my news and wanted to come to the wedding. I hadn't felt too well as I flew to Lebanon. So when I got back I saw a doctor and had a full examination. The doctor did some tests and gave me some medication. He wanted to check if there were any issues 'downstairs' so he put a small camera inside me, which went through my belly button, to have a look around. And he found a cyst. So in January 2012 I had an operation and the cyst was removed.

Following more tests, I was told I could still have children but I had more of a chance with IVF. There was hope. I was so relieved. I discussed it with Boaz and he said we'd look into it once we got to Uganda.

Boaz and I still hadn't given our notices in but we began making preparations. A lot of my possessions were with friends in Beirut where I'd once rented a flat. So I spent the next few months backwards and forwards between my job in Iraq and Lebanon; making arrangements for my stuff to be sent to Uganda. I just hoped my things would be there when I arrived.

It was getting near to my finial days in Iraq and I was busy sorting out a few bits and bobs. I gave some small things to a few of the Ugandans; clothes to the girls and I gave Wilson, who was a close friend of Boaz's, my Christmas lights – everyone celebrated Christmas at the campsite, even the Iraqis – and a small TV. He had an idea I wasn't coming back and had guessed where I was going.

"Wilson, I will see you again."
"I hope so Mama."

I also travelled back to the UK. I'd rented a storage unit in Reading where the rest of my belongings were stored. England felt strange. I hadn't been back since 2005 and it didn't feel like home anymore. I had somewhere new to call home. Boaz had suggested a shipping company in Forest Hill, London which was run by some Ugandans. So I hired a car and took my stuff there. It was over seven years since I'd looked at any of it. I threw the odd thing away but would sort them out properly in Uganda. I just wanted to get moving as soon as possible.

Unfortunately, the shipping company was very disorganised especially as the boss kept disappearing to the mosque to pray. I felt a bit ignorant as I didn't even know that there were Muslims in Uganda. They were really busy and it took ages to pack the boxes. But I had to stay and keep an eye on them just in case anything got broken or stolen. I started chatting to one of the guys and it turned out he was from a village not far from Boaz's in Uganda. So when Boaz rang to see how I was getting on I passed the phone over to him and they chatted away in their own language. A reminder of how different my life would be. I booked into a B & B in Paddington for the night, before I flew back to Lebanon to say goodbye to my friends.

Boaz arranged and followed up on most of the shipping. He was based in the Operations Room at the airport so it was easier for him to send emails and do the tracking. But I was worried about who was going to pick up my things in Uganda. Boaz told me not to worry. He had asked his old friend Isaac to collect and look after them until we arrived. He gave me his contact details and said he was always available if I needed anything. This Isaac was around my age and was a pastor. Later he was anything but Christian towards me.

I paid for everything in cash and made sure I got a receipt. I didn't know at the time how crucial that would be.

We kept Skyping, and emailing along with the odd phone call but I was exhausted to be honest. I had been in three different countries in the last four weeks and our conversations weren't that exciting. Just small talk like where will we live? Does Uganda have two pin or thee pin plugs? Should I ship my TV over or buy a nice flat screen when I get there? Some of his replies were a bit strange; it was like we were having different conversations.

25th September 2011
"I have spotted channels (I think he meant avenues) *that may channel me up to some chances of going back to Uganda earlier than expected. Leaving this undercover to know the final result. And to find out details just for your information. And keeping you in the picture as well. I love you."*

I earned more than Boaz and had saved quite a bit. I was happy to go along with his plans. After all, we were getting married. Whatever he suggested sounded okay to me.

"Now think about reserving $35,000 US dollars to buy land that can accommodate 150 cattle. It has always been my fantasy to own land."

Boaz dealt with the finances and set up a joint bank account for us in Uganda. I was a little scared about going to Uganda but Boaz always said he'd look after me. And I would like his country a lot more than mine. At the end of April 2012 Boaz headed for Uganda, ten days before me. He would find an apartment for us. It was all systems go.

I'd arranged to travel to Entebbe on 2nd May 2012 which was my birthday. All the shipping was sorted and I'd transferred funds into our joint account; around $69,000 US dollars and took the rest in cash. I spoke to Boaz the night before and told him what time my flight was due. He sounded as excited as I did and said he would be at the airport an hour and a half before I landed. I told him there was no need for that, just as long as he was there.

I was flying with Etihad Airlines and had to change planes at Addis Ababa airport which was surprisingly okay. I couldn't wait to hear his voice and tell him I was on my way. So I went to the bathroom to freshen up a bit. I very cheekily asked the cleaner if I could use her phone to make a missed call to Boaz. I couldn't leave a message as he didn't have voicemail but he would ring back once he spotted the number. In Africa it's not a problem to borrow a phone. You dial the number, hang up and wait for them to call back. And in Lebanon we did it all the time, if one of us didn't have any credit. I quickly rang his number and hung up. I had an hour and a half to kill before my connecting flight so I made sure I sat near to where the cleaner was working, just in case. As I sat there waiting, I couldn't help noticing how little she had to work with. Hardly any cleaning materials and she was using old rags and an old mop.

But as we know the phone never rang. The cleaner was finishing her shift and looked over as if to say sorry, no one called and said goodbye. I gave her a couple of dollars for her courtesy. And I sat there for the next hour worrying. But it would be alright. Boaz would be there. He was probably on his way.

As we prepared to land I looked out the window and could see how green Uganda was. Wow it looked amazing. It was a rainforest; we are landing in a rainforest! I was so excited. We flew over Lake Victoria and landed. I walked down the steps from the plane and collected my luggage from the carousel. The arrivals hall was small and I could see all the people outside so I followed everyone else and headed for the exit. There were so many people that I wouldn't be able to see Boaz so I stood by the taxi rank, away from the crowd, to make myself visible and waited and waited. I could hear that tinny 60's music coming from inside the airport, over and over again.

"He's not coming Mama," said the taxi driver. I looked at him and raised my eyebrows. But he ended up being my knight in shining armour when he offered to call Boaz on his mobile. Finally, he answered.

"Sorry, sorry, traffic. I am on my way."

He said he would only be twenty minutes but an hour later I was still there. When he finally turned up, he looked pleased to see me and gave me a big hug but something wasn't right. I couldn't put my finger on it. I admit I didn't have much of a smile on my face, and the excitement had long gone. But then this wasn't the welcome I was expecting.

"Let's take a picture of you at the airport. Like a tourist."
"Really? You have got to be kidding."

The last thing I wanted was to have my picture taken. I'd only just got off a plane for God's sake. All I wanted was to know where we'd be living and what plans he had for our future. But one thing I knew was something had changed. Was I about to make the biggest mistake of my life?

Chapter Three

The Deceit

As we drove out of the airport I noticed how busy everywhere was. The roads were narrow and there were boda-boda motorbike taxis whizzing past. Most people used them and nobody wore a helmet. The roadsides were packed with traders on all sides, selling fruit and veg along with second hand clothes.

We drove back in silence. I wasn't happy. It took an hour and twenty minutes to reach the apartment Boaz had rented. It was in the Naalya Housing Estate, just outside Kampala and part of a modern, gated compound. It looked nice. Our block was only three storeys high and we were on the second floor. There were three bedrooms, two bathrooms, a huge kitchen and massive living room. At last we were together in our new home. Boaz made a fuss and kept asking if I liked the apartment. I did.

There was no furniture except for a mattress that he had bought to sleep on. Boaz wanted us to buy everything together. How sweet. So the first thing I did was make a list of what we needed which was pretty much everything. A bed, kitchen appliances, fridge, washing machine, sofa, dining table, chest of drawers, a TV. I had shipped over brand new kitchen stuff, that was still in boxes and some nice pictures which would make it look homely. Isaac had been as good as his word and looked after my things. So we hit the shops.

Boaz dragged me down a few markets that were off the main road but all the time he held my hand and kept asking, "Are you alright?" He was so reassuring. I had a budget but it didn't last long. I fell in love with a gorgeous, Italian reclining sofa and chairs; I just had to have them. And I needed a decent bed. I suffer from back problems so I had to have a good quality mattress. We bought some lovely things and Boaz later had this beautiful coffee table made by a local carpenter. It had a glass top and the Ugandan national emblem, which is the Crested Crane, carved into the wood. The legs were figures of traditional African women but instead of carrying pots, they were holding up the glass top of the table. It looked really cool.

We shopped in local markets and paid cash for everything out of my money. Boaz insisted I carry 10,000 US dollars (that's the maximum amount of cash allowed into any country) just in case my money didn't transfer in time. At least we wouldn't starve and could shop for the things we needed. He'd said I couldn't open a bank account as a foreigner without supplying certain documents. But that was okay. I trusted Boaz. And we had a joint account. For now, I was happy. I was starving so we went to a fast food joint but the quality wasn't to my liking. I wondered if I was going to struggle with the food. But at least there was a large supermarket nearby, and it had everything we needed.

I got to know the markets quite well. Boaz would often take me to Nakasero Market which is one of the biggest markets in Kampala. It was a very busy market and a lot of ex-pats went there. You could find a huge variety of fruit and vegetables, meat and poultry. Boaz would tease me by picking up a live chicken and ask how my plucking skills were. "You could put vegetables around it and make if for my Sunday lunch." I was horrified at the thought. Yet it was just another eye opener that I would have to get used to. I'd been spoilt by the Western supermarkets.

The traders were mostly ladies and were all dressed in bright, colourful traditional clothing. They would meticulously stack the fruit and vegetables in a pyramid shape or in beautiful wicker baskets. The spices always attracted me; the different colours and smells. A lot of Asian people live in Uganda so spices are in high demand. Just the smell of the spices made me feel as if I was invincible in the kitchen and I really wanted to cook delicious dishes for my husband-to-be.

Boaz always kept a careful eye on me. The market was busy and plenty of people would stare at us; this Muzungu girl with long black hair, holding hands with this attractive Ugandan man. I think some of the men were jealous of this Ugandan with an ex-pat while the women wondered what was wrong with them. We always drew attention wherever we went. Boaz, in his protective way, would never be too far away. He'd put his arm around my waist and helped me make my way through the crowds Boaz made me feel safe.

One thing I grew to love about Uganda was the weather. Most days were nice and sunny and the temperature didn't get much higher than 24-33 Celsius. We didn't have air conditioning, and the tiled flooring kept the apartment cool on hot days. We were on the second floor and had a balcony so could keep the back door open most of the day. So a nice breeze drifted through the apartment. I loved the weather; even the rain. At night I heard the sound of the crickets. I found the noise therapeutic; to me this was the sound of Africa.

I was waiting for a certificate of 'No Impediment' from the UK Government Office to prove that I'd never been married before. Once I had that there was nothing to stop Boaz and me from becoming man and wife.

We bought the engagement ring not long after we arrived in Uganda. It was a beautiful blue sapphire. There was a sentimental reason behind the purchase. We were both into stargazing and used to refer to the late astronomer Carl Sagan. He described the Earth as the 'Pale Blue Dot' suspended in a sunbeam. This is what the Earth looks like from space. Boaz used to say that he was so happy to share the Earth with me and although he couldn't buy me the world, the blue sapphire ring was at least a piece of it.

Boaz was keen that we set up the moneylending business straightaway. One of his brothers was a lawyer so he helped with the paperwork. Boaz had no end of relatives who could help us. The company was called '*BA Financial Solutions Money Lenders*'. The 'B' was for Boaz and the 'A' for Anne, my middle name. It was also his sister's name. I designed the logo. A contract was drawn up and I was given twenty shares in the company. I didn't understand why it was only twenty instead of fifty but Boaz said as a foreigner I could only own a certain amount. Of course I was his partner and he'd change it after we were married. He also asked for a sample of my signature. As we were setting up a business account, it was just a formality.

We started looking for a car. We were renting a hire car but it was eating into our savings. I had budgeted $12,000 US dollars but that went out the window. The roads were so bad you needed a 4 x 4 to travel between the villages. They were mainly dirt tracks but at least the Chinese had arrived and were busy building bigger and better roads. So we bought a Silver *Toyota Prado Land Cruiser* for just over $20,000 US dollars. Nearly all the cars in Uganda were Toyota. They are shipped over from Japan as they drive on the left, like the UK.

We paid cash. This was out of the money I'd transferred into our joint account. It was Boaz who looked after the cash. He looked after everything. He withdrew all the money; hundreds at a time. Sometime later I realised I hadn't seen the bank cards. I wondered if we had to collect them or they were going to be sent to our address. When I asked Boaz where they were, he would say, "Don't you trust me Lisa?" Okay, fine. Once I insisted on going to the bank with him but he made me wait in the car, saying he had to do something first. He deliberately parked the car so I couldn't see where he was going. But I could see him in the car mirror making a detour into the bank. So I followed him and he did a double take when he saw me. "What are you doing here?" Before I could answer he grabbed my arm and dragged me out of the bank as if I was a 5-year-old. "I told you to stay in the car." I was very disgruntled but I didn't want to argue in the street.

We put the car in the company name so we could claim the tax back. The car was Boaz's pride and joy and he was forever cleaning and polishing it. We'd agreed that I would lend him some money to set up the moneylending business. I would also buy some land and develop my own small business. I was very excited to have a small company. At the time it all sounded great.

It wasn't long before I met Isaac. Boaz gave him this big build-up and to my surprise we got on well. He spoke very good English and was a pastor but I smelt a rat. I didn't trust him. I couldn't believe he was a pastor. Most religious people have an aura about them but I couldn't sense anything other than bullshit. And I thought he was a snake in the grass.

Boaz always needed more money and said that he wanted to get a loan so he didn't eat into my money. He decided to use the car as collateral for this loan. He was doing a project with some other people. It involved a land eviction order. I didn't know much about it but he needed me to sign some papers. So I did. If I ever asked any questions all he'd say is, "Don't you trust me Lisa?" Of course I did. But now doubts were beginning to creep in.

We had been there about two or three months. Our new life had settled into a routine. I was beginning to feel at home in Uganda and was enjoying being with Boaz. One evening Boaz was in one of the bedrooms that we had made into an office, I would often pop my head in to see if he was okay and if he needed anything. When I'd open the door, he'd shut the laptop lid slightly. He'd tell me that everything was okay; he was just trying to focus on the legal stuff for this eviction project.

One night he went to lie on the bed, saying he had a headache. I stayed and watched television in the living room. After around two hours I thought I would go check on him. He was fast asleep, sat up-right with his laptop on his knees. I couldn't help noticing that he had been drinking as there was an empty bottle of vodka on the side. Oh, I was a bit surprised as he'd said he had a headache. I gently removed the laptop; I didn't want it to fall on the floor or wake him up and took it into the living room.

The laptop was open on Facebook. It looked like it was one of Boaz's friends but I didn't know this name. We didn't have much in the way of secrets and I thought I knew most of his friends, so I started flicking through to see who this was. Then I saw a name - Dave Nicholas Katana. This Dave was posing on a motorbike. I couldn't see his face as he had a helmet on so I looked closer. But as I looked, I spotted a picture of Boaz; he was dressed in the uniform he wore at the airport where we both worked in Iraq. Mmm, this was odd. This Dave must have worked with us but I don't remember him. Hang on; has Boaz hacked into this Dave's account? But why? What business does he have with this Dave? And then I realised; this Dave was actually Boaz. No way. I couldn't get my head around it.

I checked his profile; the account was set up in February 2011. We were together by then. What the hell? And this Dave, I mean Boaz, was attracting girls. Plenty of girls. There were loads of replies from girls he 'liked'. I felt like a dagger had pierced my heart and I wanted to throw up. What the hell was he playing at? He told these girls how cute and beautiful they were. He even claimed he was an Air Traffic Controller at Beirut Airport for God's sake. Are you kidding me?

One girl stood out - Christine. There were loads of chats with her. In one he said he was coming back to Uganda soon and would love to take her out for dinner. This was the man I loved. This was the man I had left a country for; moved to another continent for. I loved this man. You can do a lot of things to me but don't dangle another woman in front of my eyes. I felt sick and kept looking round in case Boaz caught me. But I couldn't stop reading.

This Christine had a son called Ethan. That really hurt. *You are blessed to have a son.* And he would always end his comments with, *Send my regards to Ethan.* Who's this Ethan and why all this fuss? Oh, my God. Is he Boaz's son? Oh, hold on, she already had Ethan before they communicated and it seems they hadn't yet met. Phew. And then this Christine asked:

Do u have a girlfriend out there to keep u company? Sorry for being straight on.

The reply broke my heart.
God willing, we will meet in the future. Yes, I have a girl friend as in friend. Not serious yet. We're apart a lot. I just wish you was here.

I'm a 'friend am I?' Damn this stupid boy.

My whole body was shaking. At that moment I hated him. How could he? I was in despair yet I wondered if I could stand this betrayal. Ugandan women did, why not me? Was it my fault? Was I too fat, rubbish in bed?

I'm not being big headed but she wasn't even that pretty. Should I pack my bags right now but where would I go? Why had he brought me here and set up home if all the time he had all these other women? Was it some sort of game? All these thoughts were rushing round my head. Luckily Boaz was still asleep.

I had seen enough and needed to get my head together. My heart was pounding and I wanted to go back to my old habits and smoke. It was hard to imagine this was the same Boaz, the same Boaz I shared my bed with; a meal with. This was the man I had travelled all this way to be with. The same person who looks into your eyes and says they love you. He was leading this double life; putting together a harem of girls. Why? I needed to take control. I wasn't going to scream and shout. I had to keep my cool. I wouldn't tell him I knew. Not yet. I would act as normal until I decided what to do. I was wishing I hadn't seen it and actually felt I had ruined my own happiness.

The thought of him touching someone else made me sick. What should I do? I don't have anyone to talk to and it was clear I would struggle to keep control of my feelings. The stress over the next few weeks was horrible. Boaz started pushing and shoving me after I made him aware that I knew about this Dave Nicholas Katana. He tried to delete the account but he couldn't. Boaz wanted to pretend it had never happened but I had taken control and changed the password.

Boaz would leave the house early in the morning and tip toe out so I couldn't hear him. He always took the car leaving me stranded. He was obsessed with that car. Only he could drive it. To make sure he would sometimes hide the keys and once he managed to immobilize the car through the electronic key fob. I spotted the car outside and thought right, I'm off. I will go and find something to do. But, of course, the car wouldn't move.

Another time he paid the Security Guard not to let me out if I tried to leave the compound in the car. I saw Boaz talking to the guard and slipping him some money. So of course, when the Guard saw me he wouldn't let me out of the gates. I was so angry.

Quietly but firmly I said that if he didn't let me out, I would call his boss and tell him he had taken some money. "I will make sure you are fired; do you understand?" I could see he was in a dilemma and scared, so he let me out.

Boaz became moodier and if I asked where he'd been or how the business was going, he would push me out the way and tell me not to ask questions, this infuriated me. But when I finally stood up to him – you *will* tell me where you've been - he lashed out and slapped me across the face. It really hurt. I was in a blind panic. What the hell just happened? I lay on the bed crying and crying. I could see his frustration; he couldn't bear to hear me wailing and so upset. I was lying there in a ball just crying. He said sorry and tried to put his arm around me.

"Get away from me."
"I didn't mean to. I am so sorry."

He was so shocked by what he'd done that he left the house for a few hours. But the violence didn't stop. Another time he kicked my legs from under me and I fell on the floor, injuring my back. I was so shocked I burst into tears. He was on his knees begging for forgiveness, saying he still loved me and wanted to marry me, it would never happen again but it did. I'm not the type of person who will put up with cheats or violence. I couldn't accept what he had done to us. I now knew our relationship wasn't going to last and I had to get out.

From then on, if I annoyed him he would give me a slap. Once he hit me so hard across my face that he caught my lip; it ballooned to twice its normal size. Another time he throttled me so hard that I nearly passed out. I'd sometimes go to the clinic near my house but of course I lied about what had happened. I didn't want anyone to know. And he would smash up my phones or grab my handbag and turn it upside down. What little cash I had, he took. It was almost like I was being robbed by my best friend. What the hell was going on? I really didn't recognise him anymore.

Then he started disappearing. At first it was the odd day here and there but it soon became weeks. I later found out that he would go to the village but he never told me where he'd been. I don't think he had another woman in the village but now I'm not sure about anything. I'd been told that some Ugandan men had second families. I could see my chances of having children slipping away. How could I have a family now with this man? This man, who was running around with other women and hitting me.

Later I got to know one of the President's daughters-in-law. She lived nearby and I really liked her. We got on well and it was so nice just to have a friend to escape from the madness I was going through. When I asked her for some advice she said she was unable to help. All she said was that if I couldn't accept the situation than I had to get away. Oh no, that worried me. I wished I'd never asked. But I always felt that she wasn't telling me everything about her own life. Maybe she had her own problems.

I called Boaz something like thirty times a day while he was missing but he never answered. He didn't have voicemail so it would ring and ring. I would text and email but he never replied. I was lost and felt so alone in this foreign country. I would stare out of the window like a child waiting for Father Christmas. Other people might put up with this but I couldn't.

I hated being in the apartment all day on my own. So I started hanging out at a beer garden around the corner. I got to know the handy man there. He was actually well educated and spoke brilliant English, like most Ugandans to be honest. I would sit there drinking the local beer to blot out the pain. And I started smoking again. I was smoking a packet a day. That was a lot more than I ever smoked before but the stress was too much. In the end I confided in this man from the beer garden. He was sad for me and angry and worried for my safety. "Damn Ugandans," he said, "they get the opportunity and mess it all up. This is why people from the outside see us like we were nothing."

After six weeks he returned as if nothing had happened. Isaac was with him. I confronted Boaz and we had a screaming match.

I couldn't take anymore; I demanded my money so I could leave. "You want your money Lisa?" asked Boaz, "Okay, I will go and get it." He returned with $29,000 US dollars in cash.

"What's this? Where is the rest? That wasn't even half of it."
"I'll send the rest on to you. But Lisa I still want to marry you."

I was in such a rage. I didn't understand what the hell was going on. We got into a fight and he pushed me over. Isaac saw all this and did nothing. Absolutely nothing. I was on the floor screaming, hoping the neighbours would hear but Isaac just stood there, staring. He almost had a look of triumph in his eyes. Boaz grabbed me and held his hand against my mouth so no one could hear. He then threw me back on the floor.

My head was spinning. What planet was this man on? He was hitting me and using my money. Yet he still wanted to marry me. I had to get away. I took the money and packed a bag and while they weren't looking I slipped out. I ran and ran until I saw a boda-boda motorbike taxi that took me to a hotel. I didn't know at the time but my clothes were all ripped. Fortunately, the girl from the hotel helped and got them sewn up for me. Boaz had smashed up yet another phone but I'd written Isaac's number down. After a night's sleep I thought I would call Isaac. I didn't have anyone else and I knew no one else. I called him from the hotel to say I was okay. I stayed for a couple of nights. Boaz was unable to call me as he'd smashed up my phone. But he did send this email:

Lisa, am sorry. Whatever you are thinking now, good or bad, I deserve it. If you can forgive me. It's never about anyone else only us, me and you. I miss you so much. Am sorry I pushed you around. I can't imagine getting to 6ᵗʰ August without you. (This would be exactly a year since he proposed). *Please come back to your home, I made it for you.*

Isaac came over and persuaded me to come back. Boaz had promised never to lay another finger on me. We were done but I had to play the long game.

Things settled down and I used that money to buy a piece of land. At last I would have something of my own. But when it came to signing the contract for the land, Boaz had put the land in his name. "Once we are married things will make sense Lisa." I didn't argue. Boaz was very domineering. And anyway, I was biding my time.

There was a rundown house already on the plot so I got some plans drawn up. I was going to extend it and make it larger; it was going to look great. It was going to be a modest house but a good investment. We weren't going to live there. Our plan was for Boaz to run the moneylending business while I oversaw the building of the house.

The house project kept me busy but although I still felt like nobody cared, some people did. I got on well with his brother Darius, although I didn't trust him. I didn't trust anyone. Darius was Boaz's lapdog but when I told him Boaz was hitting me he said I should go to the Police. There was also my friend Enoch whom I spoke to everyday on the phone. Someone had given me his number and we hit it off. He got me a job interview at Entebbe Airport with a South African guy. It was just before Boaz took control of everything and I wanted a back-up plan. I remember Boaz drove me to Entebbe as he always wanted to know what I was up to but would never tell me what he was doing. I met up with Enoch, but the guy who was supposed to be interviewing me never turned up. The entire time Boaz just sat there staring at Enoch, refusing to speak to him. I became very good friends with Enoch and we often met at the *Lake Victoria Hotel* in Entebbe for lunch.

To get there I had to endure the Kampala Taxi Park. It wasn't a place I wanted to hang around for long but it was where I needed to be if I wanted to go to Entebbe to see Enoch. The Kampala Taxi Park was crazy, full of people coming and going, buying and selling materials and loading them onto the roofs of the taxis. I don't think I've ever seen so many people and taxis in one place in my life. When I say taxi I mean more like a people carrier. Every taxi carried heavy loads, taking them back to the villages. I would have to be quick to get a seat. I must admit the taxi drivers were good when they saw this Muzungu and always put me in a good seat, normally at the front. It made the long journey to Entebbe a bit more comfortable.

It was a 40 kilometre journey and I loved looking out the window with the wind in my hair. It definitely helped to blow some of the negativity that was surrounding my future in Uganda. Once we got outside the city the scenery was amazing. We would pass the great Lake Victoria, named after Queen Victoria, and is Africa's largest lake. This is where my journey ended at The *Lake Victoria Hotel*. It was a beautiful hotel and had a colonial look about it. Enoch would have my favourite gin and tonic waiting for me. He knew the ins and outs of my troubles with Boaz. He always encouraged me, supported me and normally he would hand me a bundle of notes amounting to 50/100 Ugandan shillings. It didn't go far but I was so grateful.

Enoch always made me laugh. Funnily enough he wasn't that keen on Boaz. And when I later told him about the violence he was so upset and angry with me.

"Why didn't you tell me? This man has run over you and then reversed all over you, and just for good measure he has taken your last penny."
"Well Enoch, I'm not sure he has as I haven't seen any bank statements."

Enoch was furious and pushed me to go to CID and speak to Grace Akullo who was the big boss. I thought maybe Enoch was exaggerating a bit about my situation.

And then there was Gary and Viola. I'd met Gary in Iraq and he was married to a Ugandan called Viola. I liked Viola. She wasn't like some of the other Ugandans I'd met, who were married to ex-pats; she wasn't a money grabber. Gary liked Boaz at first saying, "You've done well there." Gary and Viola lived only twenty minutes from us so I'd visit them regularly. I'd kind of latched on to them. Being with them helped me forget my troubles. Gary liked a drink so we would hang out at their local bar.

I would sit in the beer garden, chat and listen to some great music. They introduced me to their neighbour; "Come and meet Derek." He was another ex-pat, who'd also been in the army. He too was married to a Ugandan but no one seemed to like her much. The consensus was that she was a real gold digger who was only after his army pension. Derek often joined us for a drink. We became good friends.

I didn't say anything about the violence for a long time. But they could see there were problems. Viola was always dismissive of Ugandan men and would ask if Boaz had taken my money. She had sussed Boaz straightaway. "He is taking all your money isn't he Lisa?" But before I could answer Gary told her to shut up. "Lisa isn't stupid." But I was.

Chapter Four

Gorillas in the Mist

During that awful time, we went to the wedding of one of Boaz's cousins in the village. I didn't want to go but he kept on and on at me. He said he really wanted me there but I knew it was more about losing face in front of his family if I didn't go. They thought of me as his wife and it would look bad if I wasn't there; maybe he should take this stupid Christine instead? I still couldn't shake off his deceit. I was sure I hadn't done anything to deserve this. Boaz knew I was still upset with him and tried to lighten the mood. "Give me a smile," and I did but he told me not to bother as it looked more like a Nazi smile. That did make me laugh. Boaz came out with some funny comments from time to time. He had a dry sense of humour but under my breath I muttered, "Whatever."

It was a four-hour drive and on the way we had an argument. It began as nothing but ended up full on. We fought about everything these days. The only good thing about this wedding was it was near to the Congolese border and that meant Gorillas. I'd fallen in love with Gorillas after seeing the film *Gorillas in the Mist* with Sigourney Weaver and hearing all about them from my brother. I just had to see them.

It was still a fair old drive to get there. So after the wedding we were heading towards *Bwindi National Park*; Silverback Mountain territory. I was so excited.

But first of all we had a wedding to attend. It was being held in the garden of the bride's parents. There were lots of people and a huge marquee. I was just enjoying my time people watching. The whole set-up was really very pretty. The village houses were a mixture of brick and mud huts. It was all part of the adventure but I was glad we were staying in a hotel. The outside toilet arrangement was a deal breaker for me.

First there was a pre-wedding party. We had brought presents for the bride and groom and there were lots of speeches and more speeches. And it went on and on. I was sitting on a plastic chair in the sun, ready to nod off, when I saw this small girl sitting on the grass at my feet.

And then another one, and another one. They were getting closer and closer and all the time they were smiling and giggling. These little girls were so funny and cute. Then I realised they wanted to touch my skin; they were fascinated. It wasn't often they saw someone who was a different colour in their remote village. So I offered my hand and all three of them held it throughout the rest of the ceremony. It was one of those lovely intimate moments and made me realise how much I wanted to be a mother.

Boaz had brought bags of shopping for his Grandmother and one of his Uncles that lived nearby. I was quite honoured to meet the Grandmother as she had brought him up. She had skin like leather but amazingly, as old as she was, she was very active; still carrying wood for the fire and cooking. She had no shoes on her feet but no calluses either.

The Grandmother had a happy-go-lucky outlook on life. She told Boaz off when he made a fuss over her and presented her with a new mattress. She took my hand and led me into her mud house. I was shocked to see that she slept on the floor of this small mud hut. It was so sparse. I could see the love and kindness Boaz had for her. It reminded me of how I'd ended up falling for him in the first place.

We also met Anne who was the sister Boaz grew up with and his brother-in-law, who I knew as Mugisha. He later became a vital part of the jigsaw. Anne was very nice. I liked her; she was kind and funny.

I could see why Boaz got on well with her. Anne had five kids and they were all adorable.

One of his aunts presented me with a baby goat as a gift. She was black and white and very cute; a tiny little thing but where would I put a goat in a second floor apartment? We were heading off to *Bwindi* so would collect her on the way back. I named her *Lucy Liu*.

39

It took five hours to get to the hotel. I didn't know where we were staying as Boaz had organised it all. It was late when we arrived at the *Gorilla Resort* and getting dark but there was still daylight. The resort took my breath away. It was built on a wooden platform which was supported by massive wooden stilts. An exclusive high-end safari camp surrounded by wildlife; it was magical.

The rooms were amazing. You could lie on the bed and just look out on the Silverback Mountains. But one of the best bits was the beautiful rolled-top bath. My own bath in the middle of the rainforest. It was awesome.

Boaz had surprised me I must say, but then this was the Boaz I knew and had come to love. I think it was his mission to make sure I enjoyed my time in the rainforest. And he had gone one step further by hiring an expert Guide to take us to see the Gorillas. The good thing was that only eight people at a time were allowed to visit each Gorilla family. Protecting the Gorillas is one thing Uganda does quite well.

I was concerned about my fitness when the Guide told us we would have to climb up a hard track to get to the Gorillas. They had moved further up so it would take around two to three hours of uphill trekking. We got some walking sticks and after a safety briefing headed off.

Boaz held my hand as the ground was tricky. I was excited but also nervous about being in the rainforest. The trek was exhausting. There was a lot of climbing uphill and I slipped over many times. We had already been walking for three hours when the Rangers, who were using walkie talkies, heard that the Gorillas had shifted and were now another two hours away. Holy crap. I was struggling a bit but Boaz was helping me. And I had the walking stick and sheer determination to keep going. I had to see the Gorillas.

We moved on, crossing a river via a rope bridge. We really were in the dense rainforest. And when the Ranger pointed out piles of Gorilla poo, we knew we were close. Then we saw them, just ahead, sitting in the undergrowth. As we approached the Ranger told us to keep quiet and move very slowly. Although they were used to humans, we didn't want to scare them. And none of us wanted to see an angry Gorilla. There they were, sat in a huddle looking very relaxed. The youngsters were playing and the elders were keeping a close eye. One of them was quietly sitting there, stripping bits of bamboo. My heart was racing. I was excited to be so near. For a brief moment I remembered my brother. He would have loved us being here together. It was brilliant. Probably one of the best days of my life and it was all thanks to Boaz. He was on his best behaviour and being very attentive. This was the caring sharing Boaz that I was having a hard time giving up.

When we got back I jumped in that roll-top bath. I had mud in places you can't imagine. That bath was so relaxing. And the sound of the wilderness was amazing. I laid there until my skin went wrinkly.

I was sat on the balcony with a towel wrapped around my head when Boaz and a Guide turned up and asked if I was interested in seeing the Pygmies? Sorry? Boaz said they were in the next village and the Guide could take us. The Guide explained that the Pygmies put on a little show and there were small, handmade things you can buy. My eyes lit up. My brother used to tell me stories about the Pygmies. Pygmies are like nomads or hunter-gatherers who live in the rainforest and are very short in stature. When I was little my brother used to chase me round the house shouting, "The Pygmies are coming, the Pygmies are coming." Today it's rare to find such people living this kind of lifestyle. I had seen the Gorillas and now I had the chance to meet some real Pygmies. So I rushed round and got dressed as quickly as possible.

My hair was still soaking wet as we headed to the car. Just a short drive and we were there. There were about twenty Pygmies and I couldn't believe how small they were. Only about 4 foot and barely up to my waist. The Pygmies performed an interpretation of a day's hunting which was really good. They sang and then I had my picture taken with them. We also had a look at the souvenirs on sale. All handmade by the Pygmies.

I asked our Guide if I could say a few words. But as he got ready to translate I insisted that Boaz be the interpreter. I'd told Boaz everything about my brother and the story of the Pygmies and he had boasted that he could speak the Pygmy language. So I put him to the test. Boaz stood up and he looked very confident.

I spoke slowly so Boaz could translate. "It is a pleasure to meet you all today. I really enjoyed the show you put on.

"I learnt about you all from my brother who was in the British Army and he was posted near here and the Congo. He met a lot of you and said you were excellent tracker and hunters. He used to tell me about you when he would come back to England. Sadly, he has passed away. But I feel he is with me today so thank you for a nice memory. Thank you so much for entertaining us."

I had expected to trip Boaz up but I knew the Pygmies understood every word because of their expressions when Boaz mentioned my brother's death. They turned to look at me and there was sadness in their eyes. I asked the Guide how Boaz had done in his translation and he replied, "Better than me." That was the thing about Boaz. He was intelligent and well-read. But he could also be a right bastard.

On the drive back to the village it was raining really hard. There had been a terrible accident. Boaz said this road was notorious for accidents. The traffic almost came to a standstill and it was hard to see what was going on through the view of the windscreen wipers. As we passed a pick-up truck, there were people lying in the back covered in blankets. Their feet were dangling over the edge. I thought it was some kind of way of getting these people to the hospital, instead of waiting for the ambulance.

"No, Lisa they are dead," said Boaz.

No way. This upset me terribly. To them there was no need for an ambulance as they're already dead. They just think when you're gone, you're gone. It was an image that haunted me for quite some time afterwards.

I was feeling more and more frustrated. I was out of my comfort zone and nothing was going right. I felt like everything was closing in on me. And

I was fed up with Boaz. Seeing the Gorillas was a temporary Band-Aid for the situation and I feared the day when that Band-Aid was ripped off.

Now, as we sat in the car, I had a buzzing in my ears and felt like I was losing my hearing. Maybe I'm having a panic attack? I'd had enough of playing nice and couldn't stand being next to Boaz as he pretended to love me. I didn't want to hear his voice anymore. The haunting sound of his sweet words to other women still rang in my ears. As we approached a market town, I told Boaz to stop the car; I wanted to get out. He knew how pissed off I was with him and there was little he could say or do.

"What do you think you are doing Lisa? You have no idea where you are."
I didn't care; I needed to be by myself and by now was feeling dizzy.
"Lisa please."
"Get out my face Boaz. I will make my own way back."

I ignored his pleading. It was like his voice had become muffled to me. I grabbed a few things I needed and disappeared into the crowd. It was a busy market day and I could see a coach that would get me back to Kampala. Suddenly I spotted him following me. I weaved in and out of the crowds and took a detour. I then ran around the corner off the market square and spotted an alley way but it was like a maze. I dashed into a shop and hid behind the door. I was peeping through the cracks when I felt I was being watched.

"Mama, what you want?"

It was the shopkeeper. The old man had startled me.

"Oh, sorry."

Boaz was now at the wooden door peering in. All I could hear was my heart thumping. I put my finger to my lips and went "Sshhhh" to the shopkeeper who went back behind the counter.

"Thank you Mzee," I whispered.

If Boaz had found me there would have been another fight in a public place. I don't think anyone would have tried to help me.

As soon as he was out of sight I bought my ticket and the coach driver put me in a good seat. Once the coach was full I began my four-hour long journey home. It was peaceful and I didn't really notice anything. I was sat right at the front and just stared out the window, enjoying the view and the greenery, in between the tears. I didn't know where to start fixing my problems.

The journey seemed to go fast. It was raining hard when I reached Kampala and I managed to get a boda-boda motorbike taxi for the final stretch. When I got in I had a hot bath and went to bed. In the middle of the night I heard Boaz open the bedroom door. I pretended to be asleep. I was terrified that he might be really angry. I was surprised he was back so soon. He must have driven like a bat out of hell. But the next day all he said was he hoped I'd enjoyed seeing the Gorillas. Wow, he was so good at making me feel guilty.

Boaz continued to scare me. One day I took the car. I didn't have anywhere to go as I didn't know anywhere. I was driving around, hoping I could at least manage to get back to the house. Boaz called me while I was driving asking where I was. He was furious that I had the car and borrowed his friend's car to come and find me. I was parked when I saw him coming towards me; he looked angry. I locked the door and wouldn't let him in.

"Lisa, why are you doing this?"
"Why can't I have the car? What's your problem?"
"It's not your car. You don't deserve it Lisa."

I drove off so he chased me through the streets of Kampala. He was chasing me at high speed and calling on the phone, telling me to stop. I was terrified. I drove up on the kerbs and was going down one way streets. Darius was with Boaz in the other car. I was going down this road and Boaz had taken a detour, because he knew Kampala like the back of his hand. He came round the corner and stopped in the middle of the road. And I swear to God, if I hadn't stopped he would have smashed into me; he was revving the engine like a psychopath. By now a big crowd had gathered round and were asking what was going on? Darius got out of the car and walked towards me; I was frantic.

"What the hell is going on? I just wanted to drive the car. I don't have anything to do so I just wanted to get out of the house."
"It's okay Lisa. Calm down. Boaz just wanted something out of the car."

I really thought Boaz was going to kill me. I had never ever been so scared of anybody in my life. I got out of the car and walked away. I saw Boaz looking under the steering wheel. It turned out that he had hidden money in the car and chased me around Kampala to get it.

I was a lost soul. Thank God I still had the building of the house to keep me busy. The walls were up and all that was left was for the tin roof to be put on. The workers were doing a good job and things were going well. It was then Boaz decided I didn't know what I was doing and stopped the work. "What are you talking about?" We had the biggest fight. I was sick to death of him and he had ruined my project. I told him I needed to pay the workers but he said he would take care of it just like he took care of everything. The workers kept calling me. "Madam what is happening?" but I didn't know what was happening. Boaz never got the roof on and the rain came and all the hard work was lost. Later the house ended up looking like shit. I hated him for this. It was proof that I no longer had control of my own money or my own life.

I was heartbroken. Boaz was wearing me down. I had nothing and even the house had been taken away from me. I remember I wrote a note to myself saying I didn't know if I was trapped or being held captive. Yet sometimes he was nice and would surprise me with groceries or a meal. Once he bought a useless tub of custard powder. "What on earth did you buy that for?" But it didn't matter. I didn't even have control of my own groceries. I could only eat what Boaz bought.

He was still coming and going as he pleased. We were fighting all the time and I noticed he would come home drunk. He would smash beer bottles in front of me and then grab me by the hair and drag me through the broken glass. Another time he ripped off my t-shirt and set fire to it. There was smoke everywhere and as I tried to put the fire out, he hit me across the face, splitting my lip. He would smash up my phones so I couldn't contact anyone.

Yet he always said sorry. It was as if he hated himself for hitting me but couldn't stop. We had barely been in Uganda three months and it was like he had turned into a different person. And this person scared me.

I'd made friends with a Dutch girl called Hannah who I'd met in the *Good African* coffee shop at the local shopping mall. She'd been dating a Ugandan guy but it was complicated. I managed to build up the courage to tell her about Facebook and the girls. I couldn't actually believe I was saying these things about Boaz but it was all true. I felt bad burdening her with my problems but she was a good listener. Hannah felt sorry for me. But then she asked if he'd ever been violent towards me. I paused.

"Lisa that says it all. This behaviour is unacceptable. You know that."

I was a fool but I still had an attachment to Boaz.

"Lisa you have to contact the Police."

But no matter how much Boaz hurt me I didn't want to see him in trouble or in jail.

I didn't question Boaz anymore about Christine. What would be the point? Hannah said you either get out or forgive him. I wondered if I'd imagined it all. But not long after we got back from seeing the Gorillas he asked me to check something on the laptop. I guess he was trying to gain my trust back. I saw a Yahoo icon. I didn't know he had a Yahoo email account. I hesitated before I clicked on it. There, staring me in the face was an email from Christine. Oh no, not again.

You know what Dave, the names you call me like love and dear give me the blushes. U sound so loving, like we r a thing. U make me want to fall in love with u. Can't wait 2 meet u face to face. U know what that means. I can be so daring at times. Dave r u taking me for a one night stand?

I miss u so much. No words can express how I feel about u and us. I love the fact you are honest with me. I know you've told me 2 b strong 4 us but it's not that easy. I live for the sweet memories of us. I love us Dave and hope 2 c u soon. I am begging you to please make an excuse and meet me. I need u so badly. Am so crazy about you and I can't help it.

My heart was being broken all over again. I didn't have the strength to confront him so I left the laptop open and went round to Hannah's. I cried and cried as I told her what I'd found. She was sympathetic as always. For once I had a mobile that worked and Boaz was calling and calling. Reluctantly, I answered.

"Please come back, we need to talk."
"About what? Your deceit, your lies?"

Hannah gave me some harsh but honest advice.

"You have to stop punishing him for the mistakes he's made. Either you learn to trust him again or get out."

I had nowhere to go and no money. I still had feelings for him so I went back. He denied ever having a relationship with this Christine. "Lisa, she was fixated with me."

By now he was on his knees pleading with me. I was confused. He hit me yet he loved me. He was sorry and promised he would tell this Christine to leave him alone. After everything he'd done I still loved him.

He had broken my heart and now he would break Christine's. I later hacked into his email and forwarded this to my own email account:

Christine, I don't know how you found out my wife's name but it is Lisa Morgan and I ain't gonna change her for someone else. So do me a favour and stop all this bullshit.

But Christine wasn't getting the message:

I miss u. Please check your email daily. And if that bothers u, then ok. I miss you sooooooo much. And I love you.

His reply was cruel:
I'm sorry but this kind of talk has really created a lot of troubles for me and my wife. I beg you to stop. It's to the point of me losing my wife because of these kind of emails. And by the way my name is Boaz Asingwire not David Katana.

That must have really hurt. He wasn't even who she thought he was. And he was telling her she was the crazy one.

The disappearing act and violence returned. I was so scared that I would lock myself in the bathroom, trembling with fear. He got really nasty when I asked to see our bank statements. I was sure he was stealing my money but I couldn't prove it. And it was a hell of a lot of money; by now it was nearly $100,000 US dollars with my last salary now transferred.

If I asked where my money was, he'd say, "Lisa, you spent it," and point at the sofa or the fridge. Or, "You know you cannot be trusted with money." It was like he was trying to drive me mad.

After yet another battering I locked myself in the bathroom and called his brother, Benjamin, the Immigration lawyer. I was hysterical. "Boaz is hitting me, please come." Fifteen minutes later he still hadn't arrived. I rang him again. "I'm coming, I'm coming." When he finally turned up he took Boaz away to give him time to cool down. Some of his family felt sorry for me but he was crafty. He told them it was my fault. I was a drunk who'd spent all the money on drink and cigarettes. He also said I was out partying all the time and off with other ex-pats. He really knew how to manipulate people. The mental torture was almost worse than the physical.

I couldn't take any more so I finally went to the Police. I remember the first time they came to the house, they sat us both down. It was like a counselling session. Soon they became regular visitors but all they could do was tell Boaz off. Whenever I said he had a bad temper he always denied it and would plead innocence in front of them. He'd always say sorry officer but I have no idea what this woman is talking about. Once he even said he'd never asked me to marry him. I was deluded. I got to know the Police Officers quite well and at first they felt sorry for me but their hands were tied. So they told Boaz to behave himself and be nice to me. Domestic violence is a tricky one and it's just starting to be recognised in Ugandan law.

It didn't take long for him to slip back into his old ways. After another battering he was finally arrested. But all they did was tell him off and send him on his way. Boaz never forgave me for calling the Police. But what could I do? I told him I would keep calling them. I would never accept being punished by him. But gradually the Police got fed up with him. I would wander down to the station in tears saying he has done this and done that. The Police started to hate Boaz and tried their best to help me. They spoke to him but there seemed to be an issue with Boaz that no one could figure out. While Boaz paid the rent there was little I could do. And without money I was unable to go anywhere. If I locked him out it would be me who was in trouble. And the one thing I did understand was that now I was in trouble; real trouble.

Chapter Five

Where's My Money?

The lease of the apartment was about to end so we had to move or pay a renewal. Boaz was still hanging around and despite our differences he was paying the rent so remained in control. To be honest the apartment had always been too big for the two of us. And if I had to keep listening to those born again Christians, chanting all night, I think it would drive me insane. There were two churches not far from the apartment and the chanting and sheer volume kept me awake; it was like a bunch of demented DJ's. I don't have any objection to praying but I'm sure even Jesus and the Holy Spirit get the night off. I was glad to move just to get away from the noise.

Boaz found a beautiful bungalow just five minutes' drive on the other side of the highway. It had two bedrooms so we could still use one as an office for the business. It was a new building and in a compound with only one other bungalow. It was a lot cheaper and I liked the area. Plus, the bungalow had a lovely little garden; how I longed to sit outside and feel the grass under my feet. It wasn't quite finished and just needed some work covering the pipes in the back courtyard. It was not until after I moved in that I noticed the tin roof had been cut too short; there was not enough length for the rain to drip off, so instead, the water bounced onto the concrete plinth and then bounced back hitting the walls. Oh well, it's not perfect but neither is my life right now. And I'd rather have mouldy walls than listen to a bad version of *Bob Marley and the Wailers* all night.

Unfortunately, the neighbours kept chickens. Lots and lots of chickens and their garden backed onto my kitchen. You weren't allowed to keep that many but they didn't take any notice. If the wind blew in a certain direction the smell was horrendous.

A few nights before the move, Boaz and I got into a fight; he lost his temper and slapped me really hard. I called the Police and they came looking for him. They told him to stay away and he spent the night somewhere else. By then I was not even concerned where as long as he was away from me. A female Officer stayed and chatted with me. She was from a unit that deals with domestic family issues. She asked me if I had any money. I didn't want to tell her as I didn't know her and wasn't sure of her motives but I said yes; well, sort of.

"Mmm, you don't sound sure," she replied. "It sounds more than just a fight to me. But if you don't want to tell me at least go to *FIDA*; they can help you. I will give you the details."

She offered to take me but I said no, it's okay; I can make my own way there. I tried to stay confident, brushing off the incident with Boaz as if there was nothing wrong. But I was worried. This stupid boy was still hitting me. But the Officer had planted a seed. I liked her and she was quite cool and didn't stand for any nonsense. She didn't ask too many questions, and I don't think she needed to. It looked like she'd heard this story before. I needed to keep her close; she might be able to help me in the future if I needed her.

On the day of the move I got a text from Boaz, he told me to move all his stuff along with mine and he arranged a hire truck to come at 10 am. I was tempted to leave his things there, move alone, and forget about him. Darius turned up on the day of the move and Michael the estate agent along with a Police Officer, who I'd, made friends with. He had a great sense of humour and diverted me away from the upset of Boaz. He came to check if I was okay and if Boaz was doing as he was told. Boaz kept away alright; I didn't see him for another four weeks.

The Officer told me if I had any problems to call him, and in a few days he would pass by the new place to see how I was getting on. I took Boaz's things and dumped them in the second bedroom. I was happy to be alone. It had taken me a long time to realise I needed to fight back. There had been too many incidents where I thought right this is it. But now this was it. I am done with him. But I didn't want to waste my energy hating him. I needed to put my energy to good use, and figure out how to make things right with this stupid boy. Or make my long journey into a quick exit.

Once I got settled in I got thinking about what the Officer had said about *FIDA* and started to make enquiries. *FIDA* was an organisation that worked for women in violent situations like mine. It stands *for Federacion Internacional de Abogadas* (in Spanish). It was an organisation of female lawyers that had been founded in Mexico and now had branches all over the world. It sounded good. And best of all it was free. If they took my case I could get my money back and maybe my sanity I didn't know where I'd go but I was ready to start over, I was sick of playing the victim. I knew I had to fightback.

So I met with one of the *FIDA* lawyers who listened to my story and sounded optimistic. She was sure she could help me and even as a foreigner there was no charge. "We are going to get your money back. All of it."

She further explained, "First you need to go to your Embassy and report that you are here and that you have issues. They will advise you. Secondly, I will write a letter to Boaz inviting him to a meeting."
"Good luck with that," I smiled. "Boaz will just tear it up. Only joking!" But I wasn't.

But when she said I had to deliver it to him by hand, my heart sank and I started thinking of a plan to get out of facing Boaz. Just the thought of facing him with such a letter was detrimental to my health.

28th September 2012
Invitation for a meeting:
We act for Ms Lisa Morgan after referred to as our client. You have been in a relationship for 2 years and in May 2012 you invited her to Uganda with intentions of getting married. Unfortunately, since she got here you have been subjecting her to domestic violence including physical and verbal abuse and you have further gone ahead to deprive her of all her finances with intention to push her out with nothing.

That our client feels the relationship has been severely strained by your actions and is currently living under fear and uncertainty. Take note that your actions are unlawful and our client is entitled to seek legal redress against you in Courts of Law. On the above premise you are invited to a meeting on Thursday 4th October 2012 for an amicable discussion and settlement. Please endeavour to attend in person.

Now I was armed with a letter, I admit I felt like I'd been injected with some sort of power. This was great. It could all be over in less than a week. Now I had to sit and wait for his return, and just like clockwork he arrived at the house. I was sat on my chair, outside in my beautiful garden feeling very smug. He didn't speak to me. He just went in the house, got something and headed back out.

"Where do you think you're going?" I asked as he swiftly made his exit. "What?" he said, in his quiet voice. "Don't ask questions Lisa," and carried on walking.
"Oh yeah," well you might have to answer questions now 'smart arse.' This is for you." I got up from my chair and handed him the letter. He glanced at it. I could see the stress building up in his face and his facial muscles twitched as he clenched his teeth. As he looked up I could see his big black eyes welling up.

"What are you doing to me now Lisa?"

I was taken aback when he said this. This was not an angry voice; this was a voice of despair. Oh God what have I done? I felt bad. I stood there watching him walk away. As he got to the gate he brushed a tear from his face.

The meeting was on 4th of October 2012 and Boaz turned up on time wearing a very nice suit and tie. He always complied with what was requested from the Police or the authorities. He just had trouble following their instructions to leave me alone. He was very good at manipulating people and situations so I made sure I didn't have to leave the room for any reason; otherwise he would work his 'magic.' I've been in situations before at Police stations with dear Boaz. Whenever I came back into the room, the Police's attitude towards me had changed.

The meeting started with the lawyer speaking to him and explaining the letter and asking if he had anything to say at this point. He said no. The lawyer said it would make more sense if he would go directly to the bank and get a bank statement. Result; this is more like it. On his return I noticed that look again. That look of worry and his facial muscles started twitching.

It was the first time I'd seen the bank statement. As I studied it the lawyer did the same. The account was in his name only. I thought my eyes were deceiving me. There it was.

"Gone, all gone. You bastard," I shouted. I stood up from the chair and lunged at him. In a panic I started crying and shouting, my senses had totally left me.
"There's nothing left." Even my final salary that had been transferred over was gone. All I could see was withdrawal after withdrawal. One day he had withdrawn over $5,000 US dollars. He had looted my money. Are you kidding me?

"Where's my money?"
"Calm down," said the lawyer trying to separate me from him.
"Lisa, I drew out the money when you asked me to. What you have done with it has nothing to do with me."
"He's lying," I screamed, "he's the one who took out all the money."

Boaz looked guilty and ashamed and remained seated, burying his head in his hands. It was me doing all the hitting back now. I was so frustrated I couldn't stop crying. I cried then verbally attacked him and cried again. I felt physically sick. How could this man, this man I loved, do this to me? I wanted to be so wrong about Boaz and know the money was still safe in the account. Now I had to face the painful truth. I felt like a fool.

"Please calm down Miss Morgan," the lawyer kept saying.

Eventually she let Boaz leave. There was no point continuing.
The lawyer had seen enough and scheduled another appointment before filing for a court date. But she asked me to be patient.

But my life was in the toilet. I had no real proof about the withdrawals. It was his word against mine.

Just as things were looking up, this lawyer unexpectedly got called away to the village to attend to a death in her family. She didn't know when she would be back; maybe three weeks or so. This was not good news so I collected my files from her office. I would have to think of a plan B.

But my life was still in danger. During one argument Boaz had throttled me so hard I nearly passed out. I needed to find a lawyer of my own and put an end to this. I went through Boaz's phone while he was asleep and found a number for Robert. Robert was a private investigator and had been working with Boaz on an eviction project, which I knew little about. I had met him a few times and I was willing to take a chance with his trust. He was older and would probably take a different view of things.

I met him at a café and told him I was in trouble. I told him my story and he was horrified. He had no idea what was going on. He had been helping Boaz with the moneylending business, getting him clients. Then I told him I needed a lawyer but as Boaz had withdrawn all my money, I didn't know what to do. He was sympathetic.

"Yes Lisa, it is difficult. Lawyers here won't look at you unless you have money. That's how the innocent lose. Listen, I am owed a few favours, let me see if I can hook you up with a lawyer. Have you any money at all?"
"No, it's tied up in the car and the land I bought. The rest is gone."
"Okay don't worry, I will help you. We will meet again. I will be in touch."

In the meantime, I went to find Cecilia, the owner or the bungalow I had just moved into. She was the Chairwoman of the ladies' luxury golf club in Kololo. Her husband was a Doctor. Cecelia was well connected. I found her playing golf one sunny afternoon; she looked immaculate in all her golfing gear, nicely finished off with a pink sun visor. Cecilia could swing for Uganda by the looks of it. I got her attention and she came over.

I got straight to the point. "Sorry to bother you Cecilia but I need some help."
"Sure," she replied and I handed her the letter. I stood in silence and allowed her to read without interruptions. She understood straightaway that I wanted Boaz out of the house.

"You know Lisa, the laws are funny here in Uganda and I might not be able to get him out of the house as he has a receipt in his name. But I'm going to speak to him and I will help you." I had gained another ally.

Boaz was still disappearing and turning up whenever he pleased. One morning he was looking for his house keys and couldn't find them so he came into my bedroom and tipped my bag upside down. I was frightened he would steal my phone so I tried to grab the bag off him. But then he shouted, "I'll show you who the boss is," and left the room. He came back with a knife from the kitchen and held it in his hand as if ready to stab me. Then he grabbed me by the hair and dragged me to the front door. "Now who's the boss?" I was so scared and started screaming but I never took my eyes off the knife.

I had my keys in my hand and was frantically trying to unlock the bolts at the top and the bottom of the door. And all the time he was battering me over the head. I opened the door and ran to my neighbour Charlotte and banged on her door to let me in. Not long after I saw him leaving in the car. I sat there with Charlotte in a daze, shaking and crying. What the hell just happened and what a great impression I've just made on my new neighbour! Cecilia's efforts and hours of talking to Boaz didn't carry much weight. To me, Boaz represented the true meaning of a terrorist. Occasionally I had a visitor. Elizabeth was a Ugandan girl I used to work with in Iraq. She would make the two-hour bus journey to come and see me. She was very supportive and brought me rice and vegetables. I often looked to her for help to understand the differences in the way Ugandans did things. I was finding it hard to grasp the brutality of my situation. And how different the thought processes seemed to be. Elizabeth was brutally honest and it was a big wake-up call for me. She wasn't really surprised by what Boaz had done but she hated it. Ugandans are generally very happy and friendly people. In her eyes he was letting Uganda down. This was not the image the country wanted to create. She always used to tell me to have faith; someone was looking down and protecting me. I prayed she was right.

Another friend was Jacky. She owned a small shop on Nabe Road near to where I had moved to; you had to pass it to get to my house. She would introduce me as this new girl who lives with a Ugandan from Mbarara. This apparently was important as it's where Museveni, the Ugandan President is from. They say the most beautiful and wealthy people come from there. They also think they are superior to everyone else.

Jacky was surprised when I said I was from England.
"You don't look like you are from England."
"I am a bit Indian and a bit Columbian."

From then on she called me 'Columbiana' which stuck. As I got to know her better she would send me credit for my phone and let me pay later. Jacky trusted me. I confided in her about my situation, as it soon became obvious I was alone most of the time. Jackie knew I'd pay when I could and it wasn't my fault I had no money. I gave her some of my old clothes; most of them were now too big for me. And I invited her over a few times; we became good friends. Jacky's shop was a small brick building like a shack and sold canned food, rice, water, maze and cold juices from the fridge - when the power was working. There were a few mice running around and Jacky had this crazy goat tied up on the grass. Sometimes it would break free from its tether and run off down Nabe road. I was in fits of laughter, as Jacky screamed to the boda-boda guys, who were 'busy doing nothing' and basking in the sun. "Go, go, catch my goat," screamed Jacky. It was the funniest sight I ever saw. Seeing these young, lazy boys dashing in all directions, trying to catch Jacky's goat, made my sides hurt from laughing. My laughter made everyone else laugh. Jacky swore the goat was her pet. She called it Jessica and was adamant it would not end up in a cooking pot.

Jacky wasn't a wealthy woman but she was rich in many other ways. She was always happy and did her best to provide for her family and I admired her for that. Every day I used to walk down to Jacky's. I spent most of the time sitting there chatting with her and passing the time and literally people watching. Jacky also tried to find people to help me as she saw me gradually lose hope. She always asked me to come back later and have a drink. Sometimes I did and some of the locals would be there offering me the local *Bell Lager*. It didn't taste too nice but I sometimes felt that a drink would numb the pain. And beer was good company. Jacky was a sensible character and always insisted that Julius and Eria, two brothers who helped out in the shop, walk me to my gate.

Now I'd moved to a different area I was told to report to another Police station called Kira Road. My details had been passed on so they knew all about me and it was one step up from the small Police posts. It wasn't long before I was reporting Boaz to this police station for his disruptive behaviour. This time he had broken things in the house. I wished he would just piss off and leave me alone.

Once, when he was summoned to the Police station, he was armed with a lawyer. This guy was not very nice and I felt he was leading Boaz into further trouble. The Police Officer asked Boaz why he had brought this Muzungu to this country if he had no intention of marrying her. The lawyer nudged Boaz, as if he was giving him a signal.

Boaz cleared his throat and said, "She is deluded. I have never asked her to marry me."
"What? You bastard, Boaz. It was a very special day and I remember it well. It was the 6th of August 2011 and it's a shame you don't remember. God will strike you down for your lies."

He couldn't even look at me as I stood up. I was devastated. I burst into tears and ran out of the room. His brother Darius was Boaz's lapdog but it was obvious he had more of a heart than him. He came to check on me and put his arm around me. "Sorry about this Lisa but I have to go." Then his lawyer came out and told Boaz to forget about this stupid woman, this Muzungu. By now all the Police Officers outside were looking over. But I could see Boaz was upset by what he had just said to me. He might be acting the big man in front of other people but in reality he knew he had hurt himself more.

The three of them got in the car, *my* car and left me in tears to find my own way home. An off-duty Police Officer took pity on me and offered to take me home as he lived in my direction. I was in tears all the way home and couldn't speak. I didn't know Boaz was capable of being so spiteful.

I visited Gary and Viola a lot, but I never mentioned Boaz in any conversations.

Once, while at the bar near to their house, Boaz called me and demanded that I went home. As much as he was ruining my life he remained possessive over me.

"Where are you, who are you with?" I put the phone down on him, smiled and carried on talking to Gary.

Suddenly, out of the blue, Viola asked, "Lisa has Boaz ever hit you?"
"Don't start Viola," said Gary. There was an uncomfortable silence but then Gary asked the same question.

I hated Viola at that moment. I hated her for being right. She had been right all along. She had seen through Boaz from the start. I couldn't hide what was happening any more so I told them everything; *FIDA*, the Police, everything. Gary went mad. He rang Boaz while I was there. I tried to stop him but Gary was so angry. They had a blazing row and Gary threatened Boaz.

"If you touch a hair on her head again, you will have me to deal with. And don't you ever speak to her like that. She is not a dog and she ain't gonna come when you whistle. If I ever see you I will knock your block off."

And with that Gary hung up. Viola was not impressed and started slowly clapping. "Well done Gary. Now you've made it worse for Lisa."
He might have, especially as Boaz had a habit of recording anything you said to use against you.

Robert got back to me shortly afterwards, just like he said he would. "Meet me downtown, I don't want to talk on the phone."

I waited for him in an Indian restaurant call *The Khyber Pass*. It's really nice and I could sit outside and puff away on my cigarettes. Robert joined me outside and started discussing my next move. He told me about some legal stuff that I needed to be aware of. Plus, he said that if it was true about my money then I had to get a lawyer.

"Boaz is in big trouble Lisa for sure and he will go to jail."

Despite everything Boaz had done, I didn't want this.

"Robert, maybe you can speak to him, maybe he will give it back."

Our conversation was interrupted by a call from Boaz. He'd been ringing and ringing but I just ignored him. But then, as I looked up, he was standing there in front of us. For once I had the car and it was parked on the road. I could see it from where I was sitting. Boaz had caught Robert and me together and I could see he was pissed off. Robert waved him over, "Come and join us," but he ignored him. Then Boaz spotted the car and before the Security Guard could stop him, he jumped in the car and drove off. Well, that was the last time I would see the car for quite some time. Now Robert could see for himself what Boaz was really like.

"Okay Lisa, I can see what you're up against. Meet me in two weeks and I will bring you a lawyer. He's my friend and he will help you."

My other friend Enoch was constantly on the phone checking what was going on and if I had taken his advice.

"Lisa, listen to me, this man will leave you with nothing. Please don't wait. Go to CID and see Grace Akullo, she is the Director of CID. And go and see the IGP (Inspector General of Police). Make some noise Lisa, they will help." But I was too nervous to go.

Chapter Six

Funeral Pyre

In the middle of all this madness Derek died. He was Gary and Viola's neighbour and a retired Captain in the British Army. He had been awarded an MBE for his outstanding service. I didn't know him that well but I remember he had a great sense of humour. We would have drinks together whenever I visited Gary and Viola. He lived next door in a bungalow which was very basic. The surroundings were beautiful – really green with masses of colourful flowers. But the roads where they lived were a bit of a drama. They weren't even proper roads just dirt roads with massive potholes. The local council didn't care to fill them in and flatten them out. Damn, you could lose a small child in one of those potholes. That's where a 4 x 4 came in handy, not that I got to see much of mine.

I was on my way to see Gary and Viola when I saw Derek driving the opposite way; we both slowed down and I stuck my head out of the window to speak to him.

"I'm just coming round to see you lot."
"I'm not feeling very well. The wife's away so I'm just going to the hospital."
"I'll come and see you on the way back. Will you be okay? Do you want me to follow you?"
"No, no, you go. I will see you later."

Derek was admitted into the hospital just down the road from me. And the doctors told him he wasn't going anywhere for at least three days. That night I drank too much to drive home and ended up staying at Gary's for longer than I planned. So I hadn't visited Derek yet. Later on in the day Viola phoned.

"Lisa, Derek died."
"What? But when I saw him on the road he said he would be back later."

"He never came back."
"Oh my God."

I felt really bad. I hadn't managed to get to the hospital and now Derek had died. Gary, Viola and I arranged to go to the funeral.

My car was pretty big so I was going to drive Gary and Viola. But Boaz had done one of his disappearing acts and taken the car. I texted him, saying I needed it for the funeral. He texted back.

Get someone else to take you. That stupid boy drove me mad.

So I went to the funeral with Gary and Viola. Derek's family didn't want him buried in Uganda. They wanted him flown back to the UK but it was too expensive. So they asked if his ashes could be sent back instead.

The only places that do cremations in Uganda are Hindu temples. It was all arranged so we headed to a temple in Kampala. As we arrived, Viola spotted the widow standing by an ambulance, with blacked out windows, in the car park. She was crying and crying.

"What a drama queen and look at those fake tears."
"Viola, how can you say such things?"

I didn't really know this girl but I was beginning to understand Ugandan ways. After all, *TIA – this is Africa.*

The widow saw me and asked if I wanted to pay my last respects to Derek. Before I could say anything she grabbed my hand and dragged me up the steps and into the ambulance. I got the shock of my life. Derek was just lying there. I hadn't expected that, he was covered with a thin muslin cloth; I could see his head and stitches from the autopsy. The widow was wailing all over him.

God almighty. I'm not the best when it comes to the dead so I retreated and stumbled backwards down the steps. But worse was to come.

There was a huge metal grate and the funeral attendants were filling it with logs. Then they produced a can of ghee; it's used a lot in Indian cooking and it's highly flammable.

"Gary, what's going on?"
"You'll see."

They poured the ghee over the logs; tins and tins of the stuff. Then they brought Derek's body out. He was only covered in a sheet. Oh no. I didn't know if I could watch this. They placed poor old Derek's body on the pyre and put some logs over him. For some reason the organisers couldn't get the lighter to work so it was actually Gary and Kenny, another friend of Derek's, who set it alight. After a few minutes the heat was incredible and I had to take a few steps back. Through the logs I could see the outline of Derek's body burning. Melting. I was trying my best not to screw up my face in horror but the smoke was too much. Then the wind changed direction. I covered my eyes but I was engulfed by smoke. Gary was crying; I was crying; it was heart breaking really. It must have been hard for Gary to see his old friend end up like this.

My mum and brother were cremated. Apart from the loss of them, I didn't think cremation was a big deal. But then the coffin disappears behind the curtains and that's that. You don't see anything like this.

We stayed until there was no more to see. Poor old Derek, he had literally gone. In true British style the four of us headed to *Bubbles,* an Irish bar, to celebrate Derek's life. Farewell Derek, may you rest in peace.

That evening I spoke to Hannah and asked if she would come with me to CID. She was already more than happy to see Boaz behind bars for punishing me. But when I told her about the bank statement she really wanted to help me nail him. Hannah didn't look like me. She was blonde with white skin and extremely smart. She would back me all the way.

And I thought the Police might take me more seriously if Hannah was with me.

In the morning we headed down to CID and made a request to see the Director, Grace Akullo. When we arrived I couldn't believe that this was the Ugandan CID. It was an old building and very basic. I couldn't see computers anywhere. It seems they still do things the old fashioned way and write everything down by hand. I didn't really care what it was like as long as they got me my money and possessions back. Hannah and I had to wait hours but when we eventually got to see Grace, she acted immediately. There was no hanging around with this lady. She assigned an investigator to my case called Susan who was from the Economic Crime unit.

Susan took some brief details and all the paperwork FIDA had helped me to get. Then she told me to wait until she called me as she had to make up a case file. I couldn't wait to get started. But I hadn't finished yet. Like Enoch said, I needed to make some noise.

My personal security was a concern to me. Not only did I have to avoid Boaz in the town and going in and out of the Police stations. But now I had to start taking taxis and make sure I got back home before dark. The clapped out people carriers were the local taxis. They were designed for fifteen but I've seen a lot more being squeezed in. You were lucky to get a seat to yourself. Most of the seats had missing springs and bits of foam poking out so you could really feel it if you went over a few potholes. It was all I could afford for now until things were sorted out. It was time to look after the pennies.

A few days later Hannah and I took a boda-boda to the town. She left me at the Inspector General of Police HQ in Kampala. We were going to meet up later. I waited until I got to see the Deputy Inspector General of Police himself. John Okoth-Ochola was an older gentleman and after he heard my story and I showed him a picture of Boaz dressed in an army uniform, he started banging the desk and shouting. He made me jump.

"This woman has been robbed." And threw the photo on the table crying, "He's a fake." The Inspector was so angry he picked up the phone, "Get in here now." His secretary shuffled into his office. "Get the lawyers now."

"Yes sir, yes sir," and she shuffled out again. Within seconds two lawyers turned up.

"I called you 30 seconds ago, why weren't you here immediately? This damn Ugandan has stolen this woman's money. Get me whoever is in charge of Economic Crime at CID right now." Oh wow, I liked this guy. I sat there wide-eyed while everyone else ran around.

It was frantic. And I had front row seats. At last someone was taking me seriously. I had gone through torture and none of these other Police were listening to me. I'd been battered and had the bruises to prove it. All of a sudden I felt very emotional. This guy was helping me. At last someone was listening.

Then the phone rang and the secretary passed him the phone. "This is Deputy Inspector General of Police, John Okoth-Ochola. Get to my office now." And he slammed the phone down. Oh my word.

Within twenty minutes Susan and one of the ladies from CID were in the Deputy's office! Wow, not even I got here that fast and the CID offices were on the other side of town.

"Oh yes, I met Lisa the other day." Susan was a bag of nerves.
 "Well, get onto this now. This woman needs to get her money back. Get it sorted out so that she can get back to her country."
"Yes, Afande. Okay, straightaway Afande."

He knew this needed sorting otherwise it could get into the newspapers. And it wouldn't look good. *'Foreigner has all her money stolen and police do nothing.'* The last thing the Ugandan police wanted was bad PR. There had been a recent case where a British billionaire called David Greenhalgh was swindled out of £2.4 million by his former mistress. Known as *'Bad Black'* she'd spent it all on fast cars and partying. While little old me had lost every single penny, at least this billionaire could afford to lose a couple of million.
A few days later I met up with Robert. I was waiting in my usual meeting place, *The Khyber Pass* restaurant which was situated in the *Speke Hotel.*

The staff had got to know me and had directed me to my favourite table. I loved sitting there, it was so relaxing looking at the beautiful trees and it was the perfect spot for people watching. Plus, it serves the best *Tandoori* food ever. It was quite up-market and the tables were dressed with red and white table cloths. The staff were immaculately dressed and busy getting ready for the business people and their business lunches. I could sit there for hours and usually did.

When Robert turned up he told me that another Robert was going to join us.

"He's a lawyer and a good friend to me."

Robert knew I was sceptical and had trust issues.

"Don't worry, have a chat and if you like him you can work together on your case."

So while we waited for the other Robert, we had a coffee and caught up on Boaz's latest outrageous act. We didn't have to wait long. Robert introduced us to each other.

"Robert, this is Lisa Morgan. Lisa this is Robert."
"Hello Morgan."
"Oh it's, Lisa. But you can call me Morgan." I had an amused look on my face.

This Robert was tall, handsome and quite young. He had his own law firm called *Tumusiime, Irumba & Company*. I was quite taken by Robert after chatting with him; he was easy to talk to. I updated him on my status so far. He was impressed that I had been to see the IGP (Inspector General of Police). I was totally honest from the start. I told him I couldn't pay but I was quite capable of putting my own case together so that would save him some work. He was fine about it.

"Seeing you have opened up a criminal case already, we will wait and see what the outcome is from CID. So Morgan, update me when you get the results; it shouldn't take long. But we should think about a civil case as this will get you your money back quicker, rather than a criminal case, as this will only put him jail."

Well it wasn't long until dear old Boaz actually found himself in jail. I had called the police again after he went for me. He insisted he was the victim; that I had attacked him! But the Kira Road Police Officer could see through him and called him a liar. "You have taken this girl's money and you just want to leave her with nothing. You are an embarrassment, a disgrace." The Officer got so pissed off, he made Boaz sit on the floor, in the middle of the station, with his legs crossed. People were coming in and out, walking around him as if he was nothing.

I couldn't believe it. I was making a statement not far away so I could see what was happening. I knew Boaz would take it out on me when we got home. Unbelievably, after everything, Boaz was still able to come inside the house. I'd been told to call a Police Officer called Dennis whenever Boaz turned up. He'd advised me to lock my bedroom door and call him when Boaz arrived. I felt like a prisoner in my own home. Ridiculous!

But Boaz wasn't so cocky now. I realised he had gone from this man I loved to the immature boy he really was. But at that moment I was the one in control. I needed some air and as I walked past, I looked at him and said, "See what you've done now, you stupid boy?" When I got back Boaz had a lawyer. I didn't know this lawyer but then Boaz seemed to have a different lawyer every week. I don't know what happened while I was outside or what was said, but this Police Officer was shouting for Boaz to be taken away.

Then this Officer turned to me. "I hope you get someone to help you to take out a civil case against him."
"Thank you. I will, I will."

I remember another Officer arrived to take Boaz to the cells. Boaz would be spending the rest of Christmas Day in jail. Boaz's behaviour was so odd. Wouldn't it be easier just to give back what he'd taken?
 Darius, of all people, was also helping me. Though he was a bit too touchy feely for my liking, but he proved useful. Darius might have been

his brother's lapdog but he didn't like Boaz hitting me. He'd always said if he hits you, contact me. But what use would that do? So we had been meeting up secretly. I would protect Darius and Boaz would never know.

I tried to get information out of him to see what Boaz had spent my money on. Darius was scared and just used to say that Boaz still loves me. I never really got anything out of him apart from that. But he did say something weird. Darius said that Boaz was going to get himself into real trouble and all for nothing. What?

Boaz's Uncle Mugisha on the other hand was angry at the way he was treating me. I spoke to him a few times; he listened and felt sorry for me and was determined to get Boaz to do the right thing. But of course Boaz wouldn't listen.

But the night in the cell didn't teach Boaz anything; if anything he was back to his old tricks, I arrived back home and could feel he had been there. I had locked my bedroom door when I left but now it was open. I franticly searched for my papers, my files, bank statement, my transfer papers; registration of the car and land that I had bought; all my evidence. It had all gone. That little shit had taken all my files. At least Susan had copies so not all was lost.

Weeks passed and I didn't hear from Susan at CID. She never answered her phone and when she did she was busy and promised to call back but never did. Basically CID never updated me. I was ringing all the time but never got an answer. So I called from Hannah's number.

Susan answered and was surprised. "Oh, I have gone through the files, they're being sent to the Department of Public Prosecutions."

I had never even got to see the finished files; what was this woman doing?

"Well, how long does that take?"
"Sorry, I don't know."

I was so frustrated that I spent most of my time at CID asking about my file. I got on with the secretary there quite well and we'd have a laugh. I was always in the waiting area with about ten other people squeezed onto a sofa waiting to see this Susan. I could see the secretary felt sorry for me and always asked, "How are you Morgan?" Ugandans are quite formal so nearly always called me by my surname.

A lot of journalists hang around the station looking for stories. I was there so often they could see that there was something going on with this Muzungu. This one journalist always spotted me and tried to get close but the secretary shooed him away. He worked for this sleazy newspaper called *Red Pepper. It* was full of scandal and half naked ladies of the night.

"I'd like to get to know you better. Can I write about you?"
"I don't know," I replied. "Do I have to take my clothes off and dance around a Minister's knees?" The secretary thought it was hilarious.

Robert called me. "How are we getting on Morgan?"
"We are not. I've just got home having spent all this time at CID and I never saw anyone. But I saw the car. The car was parked there, 'my' car, so something is moving."
"But Lisa, Susan never updated you about the car?"
"No."

Robert didn't sound convinced that things were moving.

"Okay Morgan. We should start the civil case proceedings. Come and see me next week as I'm in the West of Uganda for the rest of this week."

But I was still frustrated. And people talked. I'd heard rumours that Boaz had been seen at the Department of Public Prosecutions Office. I didn't really understand what he would be doing there or even what this place was. I would ask Robert when I saw him.

Things just weren't moving fast enough. I'd had enough. Thank goodness I had Enoch and Hannah to spur me on. They'd told me to get in everyone's faces; not to give up and go to the very top; insist on seeing the Inspector General, which I had. Now it was time to see the big boss. So I headed back to the Inspector General's offices to complain again about my case and my lack of protection from Boaz. This time I asked to see the Head of the Ugandan police; I didn't really know who he was. All I knew was that he was called Kayihura. He wasn't there but would be back later. "I'll wait."

A lawyer called Isaac was also there. He had been in Deputy John Okoth-Ochola's office when he was doing his War Dance. Isaac was funny and supportive but a very busy man. He said he would call me when he saw the Inspector General. So I went outside to puff on a cigarette.

I was chatting to a military driver who was washing his truck, when this big 4 x 4 with blacked out windows pulled up. The driver got out and opened the back door pretty sharpish. I could tell whoever was in the car must be important. Then a tall, well-turned out man in Military uniform got out. Suddenly the guy washing the truck said the General wants to see you.

I looked around. "Me?"

And with that this General started making gestures for me to come over. I was in a flap and quickly put out my cigarette.

The guy washing his car was highly amused as I stumbled about, collecting my files and breathing on my hand, hoping I didn't stink too much of cigarette smoke. When I got to the car, I read his name badge; Kayihura. Oh. Kayihura. This is the top man. The man I was waiting to see.
"Hello Sir, hello General."
I wasn't sure if I should shake his hand or bow. I was very nervous.

 "Are you being looked after?"
I didn't really know what to say so just said yes. Well no! I don't know!
He was very nice and very polite; a serious looking man, he asked me to

71

walk with him. So we walked through the corridors. Everyone was looking. I struggled to keep up with him as he had extremely long legs.

"So why are you here?"
"I am here Sir because I came to this country to be with someone and I have got into trouble with my relationship; and he seems to have stolen all my money. I'm worried for my safety as he still insists on coming to the house and can be violent towards me."
"Mmmm. Okay, I am very sorry but we are going to sort you out. Sit in that office and speak to my assistant and tell him everything."

And Kayihura made it clear to his assistant that he wanted an update. So I told him everything. I found out later that Isaac, the lawyer, got Boaz arrested and wanted to detain him, to get him out of the way, and protect me from his violence. I was shocked when Isaac later told me that Boaz had confessed he had done wrong and broke down in tears.

"I love Lisa; she is everything to me. I hate myself for the things I have done to her but I am under pressure. I have mixed with the wrong people and I have had bad advice. I need to go and speak to Lisa and I'm going to fix everything." Unfortunately, a Police Officer believed Boaz and released him. Boaz fixed nothing and did nothing. He deserved an Oscar for his performance.

I'd got to know this Ugandan that had worked in Iraq and he introduced me to his friend who said he wanted to help me. Yeah they all say that. Anyway I told him my situation and that I was in a lot of trouble.

"Come with me, I want you to meet my friend Betty." Betty worked for Interpol. I liked her immediately. She sounded like she knew what she was talking about. We chatted for a while and Betty said she would speak to someone who could help. I was so tired of all this. Everyone wants to help but nothing ever happens.

Then Betty asked, "Lisa, where is your evidence now?"
"Well he stole my copies but the rest are at CID, along with the car."

"Go get it now. You need to get your file back."

"But it's safe there isn't it? It's locked in her drawer."

"Lisa, go get it now, don't trust anyone."

"What?" Betty had got me in a panic.

I called this Susan and I told her I was coming to see her but she told me not to come now. I didn't understand why. I told Betty what she'd said.

"Go Lisa, go now." Betty got me a boda-boda taxi. If it wasn't for Betty, I'd never have caught Boaz and his brother red handed.

Chapter Seven

Get Your Hands Off

As the boda–boda turned into the police station I spotted my car. It was still parked there after all these weeks. I could see the door was open and as I got closer I could also see that someone was inside. I quickened my pace to see who and what they were doing. Up until now the car had remained spotless; more than I could say for *Bad Black's* once immaculate Range Rover Sport that was parked near mine. There wasn't one body panel straight and it was totally vandalized.

As I got nearer to the car I could see it was Darius, Boaz's brother, sat in the driver's seat with the engine running. He was in my car; 'my car'. "What the hell are you doing?"

Darius was shocked when he saw me. "Oh, I am just starting the car." He realized what an idiot he'd been and looked like he was going to burst into tears.
"Get the hell out of my car Darius."

Darius said, "Boaz is around and has gone to get credit for his phone."

"I don't give a shit where he is. Get out and give me the keys. Darius don't get involved."

But he stayed in the driving seat as I went round to the back door. I opened it and on the backseat was a big brown envelope with my files peeping out. What the hell? I knew they were mine. I recognised the plastic folders I'd brought over from England. You bastard. I grabbed them. But Darius tried to snatch them back. "No, Lisa please they are mine." At that point I knew he was in on it. Why would he say "They are mine?" You wouldn't say that unless you knew what was in the envelope. Darius was pulling and pulling but no way was I letting go.

"Please Lisa, don't."
"These are my files." I screamed.

I held on for dear life. He wasn't getting his hands on them. I pulled so hard that they slid from his fingertips. I ran towards the CID building, clutching the files. I was raging. I couldn't believe what just happened. My heart was racing. That bloody Susan had let him have access to my files. She told me she was sending them to that Prosecutions place. God knows what is missing or what would have happened if I hadn't got there in time. What would the story be now? "I am afraid the car got broken into and the file is gone." That bitch.

I ran as fast as I could. I was still scared Boaz would catch me. I dashed into the waiting room of Grace Akullo, Head of CID. Her secretary was there along with a bodyguard. "What's wrong Morgan? What's happened?" I told them, they were shocked. "Oh my God, this is very serious." I asked if they would help me and come as witnesses when I confronted Susan. "Yes, we will help. It is our duty Morgan."

We got to Susan's office; she was shocked to see me and the other two. She was even more shocked to see me with this envelope. Susan had obviously put my files in this big envelope to disguise them. I sat down and placed the envelope on my lap.

"I've come to collect my files Susan. Can I have them?" She didn't know what to say; I sat and waited for an answer. She was a great big blundering mess. I, on the other hand, was calm and cool. I wanted her to suffer like I had suffered all these months. I was enjoying this.

"Susan, shall I help you? Shall I tell you where I found my files?"
 "No, no I know where you found them. I put them in that envelope and then put them in your car." She smiled nervously. "Look around, it's not safe in my office. I was keeping them safe."
"Really? They're not safe in your locked drawer, in your locked office, in a locked building? Can you tell me what Boaz's brother was doing in my car with the engine running? Trying to steal my files maybe?"

Her phone started ringing.

"Answer it Susan. I'm sure it's Boaz looking for a shoulder to cry on."

Sarcasm had never seemed more appropriate. I had got her. And with two witnesses to back me up she was toast. Susan started shouting and abusing me but I wasn't listening. I got up and told her that she was very unprofessional and a waste of Ugandan money. Now I wasn't going to be messed about with anymore. I would fight back even harder.
 I addressed the bodyguard. "Grace Akullo office, please."

The bodyguard took me straight to her office, knowing that my head was ready to explode. He told me, "Morgan, take a deep breath." He bypassed about five other people that were waiting to see Miss Grace, as I called her, and brought me straight in to see her.

I told Miss Grace what had just happened. "My goodness." Then out the window we both saw Boaz and a male Police Officer talking.

"Is that him?"
"Yes, that's him."

Miss Grace apologised and said she would assign another CID Officer to my case. She directed me downstairs to a lawyer and told me to make an official complaint. The secretary and bodyguard would do the same. I refused to give my files back until I got another investigator. But I could already see there was stuff missing. I was so angry with all of them now. I didn't know where all my papers were or if my evidence had been sent to the Prosecution place or not. I had no idea what was going on; they had disorganised me.

Boaz had been trying to destroy my evidence, all under the noses of the police. He'd probably bribed someone to turn a blind eye. The corruption in Uganda amongst the Police especially is unbelievable; money talks. I think he must have given some sob sorry to Susan as she was fighting his corner well. Or my money was lining her pockets.

When I met up with Robert and I told him what had happened, he was totally shocked. "Oh my God; Oh my God. So much has happened to you Morgan but you're a fighter." Robert found me amusing. He laughed like the British comedian Lenny Henry. And was impressed by my investigation skills.

"Are you sure you're not related to James Bond?" he laughed, "but seriously Morgan, we need to take action."

Later he drafted a letter to Miss Grace formally recording everything that had happened to me.

"If the police are not going to arrest him, we have to stop messing about here Morgan. I'm going to file a case to the Civil Courts but you have to get the rest of your evidence. At the moment there is no proof that you were planning to marry. Without that we don't have a strong case. It's still his word against yours. Find out what you can Morgan, we need something."

Head of CID Kabuli
Miss Grace Akullo

Due to the circumstances in which you are aware of. Ref: Lisa Morgan & Boaz Asingwire Case of Fraud.

Due to unfortunate events that Miss Lisa Morgan has endured from Mr. Boaz Asingwire since May 2012 to date, it is with much concern that Miss Lisa Morgan is still subject to attacks from Mr Boaz in the home. Several attempts and interventions have been made by Kiwatule Police station to prevent and assist Miss Lisa Morgan to keep her safe and uninjured, while living under the same roof as Mr. Boaz. But these violent attacks within the house sustained by Mr. Boaz are still on-going. My Client, Miss Morgan, is in great danger and finds herself in a situation that when even she calls for help to the Kiwatule Police the local post, they either don't turn up or they don't answer the phone.

On one occasion my Client again sustained strangulation, biting, hair pulling and bruising to her left elbow.

Although she calls the Kiwatule Police station they fail to answer her call or follow up. She feels that the police are not going to assist her and she is left open to more violence. My Client is suffering from great stress since being in Uganda and the treatment that Mr. Boaz has subjected her to. It is of great interest that she leaves the home along with her possessions; where she is living, for her own personal security. This is to prevent more attacks accruing. It is imperative that Miss Morgan's address will not be revealed to Mr. Boaz, but she will leave a telephone number for the police where she can be contacted while the cases are resolved.

I hope that you appreciate my concerns for my Client is paramount and I don't wish for her to continue any further violence that could lead into a fatal situation.

Amazingly, the day before Robert drafted this letter, Boaz slapped a letter on the desk of Miss Grace. She gave me a copy.
Request to Stay Alone
I cannot keep staying with a person who continues to harass me with insults and abuses me with insults and abuses yet there is currently nothing we share in common. This is a person who comes in every night late and sometimes drunk and begins to abuse me. This is a person who has started hiding and concealing some of my personal properties and hurts me with horrible words.

She claims she does not have the money, but where does she get the money to invest. Outings, drinking and smoking daily. She is falsely creating a hideous image against me. Unknown injuries she has on her body which I don't have knowledge of but blamed on me. I contacted the Kiwatule Police but it turned futile when she became abusive towards me in presence of the police. I request this matter be looked into as Morgan Lisa Anne is crossing lines of decent human behaviour.

Me? I was the one, "crossing the lines of decent human behaviour." Really? Now everything started to go wrong.

I was unsure how long I could survive on the little money I had left but somehow I remained lucky; if you can call it that. The British

Ambassador's chauffeur got to know about my story and he would bring me bags of shopping when he was passing. At least I could re-stock those empty looking shelves. I was amazed by the generosity. But I needed money to get out and about. I was scared to get taxis after I was tricked one day. The taxi door was jammed and I had to push the door to open it. As I pushed a hand was in my bag. When I realised what was going on the driver kicked me out. It was dark and I wanted to cry. I was so scared.

I had to start asking my friends back in the UK or US to help me. I hated begging for money. I was ashamed but I couldn't manage like this. I was already eating the local food to save money. I would go to a place near Jacky's shop with my plastic container; this old lady had a big tin pot cooking over an open fire. She filled it up with sweet potatoes, meat and gravy. You could see the locals looking and talking about me as this was not where a Muzungu would normally eat. I didn't know what meat it was but you just have to close your eyes and get on with it. It was food, it was a dollar and this was my life. Either I try harder or want for less. And physically, I didn't have the energy to try any harder.

Days turned into weeks and there were still no signs of my case being seen by a judge. I would call Robert every day but there was still no date. I'd spend hours lying on the bed sobbing. One time I was lying there during a thunder and lightning storm. When it rains in Uganda it really rains so when the heavens opened the noise was tremendous and the sky lit up. Maybe the rain will clear my head? Wash away the pain. So I took off my shoes and ran out to the garden. I held my arms outstretched and let the rain come crashing down on me. The downpour was so strong that it hurt my skin but I didn't care. I was soaked through and my feet were covered in mud. And then I started laughing. It was as if I was possessed. I stood there and laughed and laughed. But then the laughter turned to tears. Knowing I would still have to face the same pain the next day. Nothing's changed no matter how much I enjoyed this rain now, the pain will soon follow.

I collapsed in the darkness exhausted, with the rain still beating down on me, and sobbed but no one came, no one heard me. I was frightened and penniless and felt so drained. I didn't know what day it was from the next. It was like I was in a permanent daze. And I had never felt so lonely in my life.

I used to try to keep myself busy by trying different hairstyles, painting my nails and putting on make-up. But when I looked in the mirror all I could see was ugliness.

I'd walk down Nabe road and passed the two brothers' house, Julius and Eria, but they were out so I would walk to the Metroplex Shopping- mall. I had to run across a busy highway and walk down an embankment; then head down a small track to get there. I remember once my flip-flop came off my foot, as I ran across the highway. I was on the other side of the road hopping around. Fortunately, a boda-boda guy stopped and risked his life to retrieve it for me. It was at moments like this I could at least laugh at myself. I was still me; just a bit broken, that's all.

There were some good people who tried to help me. Robert, my lawyer, even gave me money to get home safely from town after our meetings. Who'd ever heard of a lawyer who 'gives you money'! Once my begging letters went out my friend Randy from Texas and 'William' in Utah sent me money from time to time, along with another friend Scott Veitch, from the UK. He sent me £200 which meant I could eat and get around for at least three to four weeks.

It was such a nice sunny day and with the money I had just received, I headed for the supermarket. But I was still crying so wore big sunglasses to hide my tears. I'd pick up things in the supermarket that I liked and put them back. I used to take a calculator and add up everything before I got to the counter. Once, I was so embarrassed when the till operator added everything up and I didn't have enough to pay. So I had to put things back. I made out that I must have lost some money from my pocket but I hadn't; I just didn't have it. This was how fast my life had changed. The girl who earned $350 a day; the girl who honoured the promise to get married. The stupid girl who messed up her life.

I broke down in the supermarket a few times. Once a Security Guard came over as he thought I had fallen over but I was just doubled up in tears. To think it wasn't that long ago that I used to shop hand in hand with Boaz. Now he was nowhere to be seen.

All I had to look forward to was another long, long boring night. I had watched every single 'Who wants to be a Millionaire' on the TV. I had won millions by remembering all the answers from the last time I'd watched it but, ironically, I didn't have the million-dollar answer to get me out of my own mess. If I didn't have money to keep up the subscription for the sky channels I would just curl up in my chair and stare at the empty screen.

Darius called a few times but I was still mad about that car business at the CID HQ. He wanted to meet with me. Keep me posted. I didn't really want to know what his brother was doing or even ask questions but I went to meet him. We chatted a bit but he wanted more saying he missed me. Oh my God. I wanted to be sick. Then he got a call. "I have to go but please wait for me here. I will come back." So I waited.

He was back in an hour. "It's your lucky day."
"I doubt that."
"Look at what I have here." Darius looked very smug as he handed me an envelope.

When I looked inside I couldn't believe my eyes. Inside were the bank statements, letters and transfer receipts; even Boaz's passport which he'd accused me of taking. Boaz had given them to his brother to keep safe. Ha! We went to photocopy everything. Now I had some crucial pieces of evidence to add to my case file. I couldn't wait to tell Robert, my lawyer.

After all the troubles with Boaz he still turned up at the house from time to time. If I couldn't legally get him out the house, then at least I could avoid him if only to keep myself safe. He once said that if he wanted to take my money he could. He would be gone and never be found.

I guess he had a point. So why was he still here? Maybe I was wrong about him? Was I missing something?

I could never bring myself to hate Boaz even though he deserved it. I always kept the faith and if there is a God then this would be the perfect time for him to make his judgement. Funny how you think you're in control of your life but actually life is in control of you. Maybe life is really designed and mapped out for us all. But this was not my dream; this was a nightmare.

I wouldn't see Boaz from one day to another. But then he would just pass through to get a clean shirt. Sometimes he would stay in his room or he would turn up with food for himself and eat in his room. Yeah, great. This would anger me as I hadn't eaten a good meal for days. Strangely enough Boaz would sometimes bring shopping and cook a full dinner; vegetables, meat gravy. He would bring me a plate while I was sat watching TV. We didn't ever speak but I was polite and thanked him. This way the hitting stopped and I accepted his path was different to mine even if his path was a path of deceit, deception and lies.

Ironically he would leave the house on a Sunday morning with his Bible clutched in his hand. I would watch him through my net curtains as he reached the gate and disappeared out of my sight. It was hard to be in the same house with the one you wanted to love but knew you couldn't. It was equally hard to see him leave and not know who he spent his nights with. What happened to this boy? Had he really sacrificed love for money?

Robert, my lawyer called. "Morgan, how you holding up?"
"I'm okay," I replied. But I was really feeling the strain and the waiting was killing me.
"Listen Morgan, it might take a while to get a Judge, like six to eight months. Can you manage?"
"No. Robert you have to help me. I can't continue, please."
"Yes, yes I am going to help you."
I started to cry and cried and cried. By now I was hysterical. "Please Robert, help me, I beg you." Robert put the phone down. I guess it was hard for him to listen to my pleas.

Chapter Eight

Moving Things Along

It was 14th of February 2013 and I had just arrived home. The house was in darkness and Boaz was on his way out. As he passed me he smiled but didn't say anything. When I walked into the living room there was a candle burning and two bars of chocolate, a rose and two cards. I opened them both but they didn't say much. I was already so back and forth with my emotions that he must know he'd never be able to get me back. I wasn't going to be with a man who raised his hand to me. And it wasn't because I didn't love him. I think I will always love him; crazy as that sounds. I just didn't like him that much. I tried to call him to thank him for my cards and flowers but he never answered the phone and he stayed out all night. In fact, I didn't see him for weeks. I threw the cards on the burn pit and watched them go up in flames.

I started to become withdrawn. I wasn't shouting anymore and hardly spoke. I ignored calls from my friends Hannah and Enoch as I was sick of listening to myself. I felt I had no way out and the conversations were always the same. Boaz started to call me, he never called me. Maybe he realised I was weak and he was missing his playmate. When we were together, and I'd call him, he never answered his phone and I had to listen to that stupid *Diamonds in the Sky* ring tone of his. Even now I can't listen to that *Rhianna* song. I really didn't care for his calls. It was too late to rescue the situation; it was too late to go back.

I started to think that maybe it was better if I was out of the way. At least one of us would be happy. I just couldn't survive this. I had no energy left. Boaz had finally tipped me over the edge. I wanted to sleep; I didn't want to feel this pain anymore. The only person I wanted to see was my brother and if I had to kill myself for that to happen, then that's what I would do.

I sat in front of the mirror that Boaz had bought for me; the one with the carved love heart on it. I said goodbye to this face and gave thanks for the healthy body I'd been given to make this journey. I cut off my hair and placed a lock of it on the bedside table along with a picture of Boaz. I put on my favourite piece of jewellery and the dress I had chosen to get married in.

I crushed up a cocktail of tablets plus sleeping tablets and swallowed them. I then sent Boaz this text:

Your lies are worth more than my life. Call my sister when it's over. She will know what to do with my body.

Then I lay on the bed, and drifted into sleep, hoping never to wake up. But I did wake up. I was drooling from the mouth and Charlotte was screaming, "Muzungu, Muzungu, wake up wake up."

Boaz came in and was shaking me, slapping me around the face. He had also gone to the Police station and dragged a female police officer with him after he couldn't get through the gate as I had changed the padlock that morning and only Charlotte had a key. "Please Lisa, wake up."

He had called Charlotte at work and asked her to, "Send me the keys with a boda–boda. I need to get into the compound." But Charlotte was so protective of me that she said no; she didn't trust Boaz. She told him to wait; she was coming.

Now Boaz was begging me. "Why are you doing this? Please Lisa, do not hate me, I am sorry for what I have done. I am going to fix everything."

But Charlotte knew exactly what was going on and she was not pleased. She wanted Boaz to leave and leave for good.

I didn't feel too good afterwards and threw up most of the night. But it made me realise that despite the sheer pain of my situation, I didn't want to die. I wanted to live. I wanted to fight back. It was like my brother was screaming at me in his Sergeant Major fashion; telling me to wake up and pushing me back into the living world. Boaz's tears didn't last long. By the end of the day he reported me to the Police, stating that he could not be held responsible if I took my own life.

I didn't know that someone from the very top had made an order for Boaz to give me money for my upkeep. It wasn't until Dennis, the Police Officer who was trying to help me, came round with a letter for me to sign and 50,000 Ugandan shillings; that's about £10. I signed it but I'd be lucky if Boaz kept up the payments. Ironically I was now signing for my own money that he had taken from me. The Police could see I was suffering but couldn't do much else.

Now I wanted Boaz out of the house. "It's better you leave and we are separated. All I do is sit here and all I see is you walking in and out. At least this way we might get over each other. I have lost everything being with you. It's better I lose everything and not see you."

He just looked at me. Then he answered his phone. He was always on that bloody phone. Whispering; sniggering; plotting. But I carried on.

"When I no longer cry over you Boaz, you will know you're in trouble. If it's money you want, you can have it. You only had to ask, you don't have to fight me for it. But this money will only turn to ashes in your hands because it doesn't belong to you."

Boaz sighed, as if he felt sorry for me. "I am not moving out completely. I can come and visit. "
"Visit for what? A cosy cup of tea?"
"Yes, yes exactly."

He had to be kidding. I just didn't get him. He had spent the good part of a year turning me against him. Yet when he finally decides to move out he's talking his way back in.

But Boaz did finally move out. I didn't know where to but Darius told me he was staying with a sister called Rebecca. But he couldn't go without one last spiteful act.

I walked into the living room and the TV was gone. He had taken my damn TV. I didn't cry this time. I called and texted him, calling Boaz all the names under the sun. The cost didn't matter. It wasn't about losing another possession. No, the TV offered me escapism. It took me away from everything. Shit, now I had nothing. No money, no TV, nothing. He even took my bikini and a flag from Iraq that my co-workers gave me, along with my sapphire ring; all gone. But then I thought okay two can play this game. Let's see how you like it.

Robert was always cheerful. "Morgan how are you? How is Kiwatule and how is Nabe road? Listen I need you to write a letter to the Judge to move things along. I have drafted a letter and I need you to come to the office and have a look."

May 31st 2013
Dear Worship
I am writing in great urgency that my Client Lisa Morgan, the Plaintiff, who is a British citizen, is seen that her case is dealt with great urgency. She has no means of financial support, nor a valid Visa. The Defendant Asingwire Boaz has vacated the home and has left my client with rent, water and electricity bills. My Client is suffering from emotional stress. She has put her cries in the attached letter. And she wishes to leave the country Uganda as soon as possible. I kindly request for the earliest possible date to get her matter resolved
Hoping for your positive response
Yours Faithfully

I, in turn, wrote from the heart:

I'm writing to you to plea that my case is dealt with great urgency. I am a British national and arrived in Uganda with the intention of getting married and setting up a business. I transferred my savings over to a joint account in Uganda. Since my arrival in May I have faced many concerns re: my money not being accounted for. I have suffered as the defendant continues to abuse me mentally and physically. As he has now spent all my savings I am not able to move anywhere safe. I have to borrow money or ask for food to live.

Some days I don't eat, while he goes out all day and comes back drunk at 2am. I am frightened for my life as he has battered me around the head so bad that my back tooth came loose and eventually fell out. I want to leave Uganda as soon as possible as I can't take the stress and abuse anymore. The longer I stay the longer my life is in danger. Please don't allow me to suffer any more than I have to. I will be deeply grateful if you can do your utmost to see my case as urgently as possible.

Robert was hopeful that this would get things moving. "Let's sit and wait Morgan. Why don't you go and visit your friend Gary for a few days and I will call you when I have some news."

So many people were trying to help. After the attempt on my own life Dennis, who was a local Police Officer who had tried to help me before, came to my house. He was worried about my safety.

"I'm so sorry that you are going through all this, I need to help you. I have written a letter and I've sent it to higher authorities."

March 21st 2013
Senior Probation and Welfare Officer
Kampala City Council Authority

Re: Urgent Welfare Complaint of Party in Police Case
The purpose of this letter is to bring to your urgent attention the precarious situation of a British national, Ms Lisa Morgan, presently domiciled in Kiwatule-Kampala.

In May 2012 Ms Morgan (Party A) permanently moved residence to Uganda from Iraq to get married to Mr Boaz Asingwire (Party B). As part of this transfer process winding up her affairs in Iraq, Party A transferred her personal savings of over $60,000 (sixty thousand US dollars) to Party B's Uganda bank account with the expectation that she would open up her own account upon arrival in Uganda and Party B would transfer the money to Party A's account. However this did not transpire.

Since September 2012, the relationship between Party A and Party B has degenerated substantially to the point that it has required Police intervention in the matters of domestic violence and fraud.

The case of fraud is being investigated by CID HQ. During the on-going investigation it was verbally agreed that Party B would provide regular financial support for Party A's upkeep; however the amount and period of regularity were not specified. Party A has repeatedly complained that the small amounts have not been able to support a minimum living of survival and have contributed to the mental and emotional cruelty and torture meted out on her along with the incidents of domestic violence.

We wish to bring this case to your priority attention for your urgent intervention to ensure that a formalized agreement of reasonable upkeep is put in place and adhered to, of which failure to do so would result in measures of law enforcement.

We would be most grateful for, and look forward to, your speedy intervention to reduce further difficulty or complication to the Parties in the case.
Yours faithfully
C/ASP Onyanga Dennis

So many people were beginning to realise that my life was in danger.

I needed to get away and do what Robert suggested. I'd get the bus and stay with Gary and Viola for two or three days or until Robert called me to tell me to come back. They had moved to a place called Jinja, which was further away, heading towards the border of Kenya and took me around two hours in a taxi.

I loved the journey and loved watching people getting on and off. And the odd smile and interaction from the friendly people made me feel relaxed. Once I accidently ended up with someone's chicken on my lap. It made me scream. People laughed and the driver told the man who owned the chicken to stop frightening the Muzungu. It's a remarkable place Jinja. It sits on the Northern shores of *Lake Victory* and it has a hydro-electric dam at *Owen Falls*, near the city. It's also a popular place with backpackers as there is so much to do; River Nile Cruises, rafting and there's so much wildlife to see. Gary, Viola and I used to go a local bar there called *2 Friends* which was popular with ex-pats.

I got a call from Robert but it wasn't the call I was expecting. He said Boaz had rung and was asking where I was. Robert wouldn't tell him.

"I hope your place is secure Morgan."

The police also called while I was with Gary and Viola.

"Are you Lisa Morgan?"
"Yes."
"We just want to know where you are."
"Why?"
"Your husband Boaz just wants to know that you are safe and would like you to come home."

Unbelievable, he's moved out and now he's concerned about me? Wow the tables are definitely turning. Husband indeed! Finally, I got the call.

"Morgan, we have a date. I spoke with the clerk today and a Judge called Kabiito is taking your case. Get back here on Wednesday. We can meet and prepare. Okay?"

I was so happy, "Yes, yes." And Viola was impressed.

"Wow, first class service."
"What do you mean?"
"Kabiito is a good Judge Lisa."

But I still had to be careful. A guy from CID HQ called me, insisting I had to come down to the station.

Something wasn't right so I asked Robert, my lawyer. "Delay, delay for as long as possible." He didn't like the sound of it either, "don't go anywhere Morgan, unless I'm with you."

So I called Joshua. Detective Assistant Muwanga Joshua was my newly assigned investigator. He was very nice and I felt I could trust him. He told me that Susan had at last sent my file to the Director of Public Prosecutions (DPP). Joshua was there just to assist me to the end of the criminal investigation.

"What does he want?"
"A statement about Boaz's email."
"Keep away from him. If you go down there, he could arrest you and put you in jail."
"What?"
"This guy is not to be messed with."

I was terrified. Joshua said it's possible he will arrest you; they can put you in jail in Uganda without a second thought. I guess Boaz was feeling the pressure and didn't like the taste of his own medicine, so that's why he'd made a complaint. Putting me in jail would get me out of the way and delay my court case.

Yet, after all this, Boaz would still call me, asking to meet up. I was feeling more in control now and I could see kinks in Boaz's armour appearing. "Come to the house then," but he wouldn't. He had stolen the TV and thought it might be a trap and the Police would be waiting for him. So instead we'd meet up at the supermarket. I asked him what he wanted.
"Nothing, I just want to look at you."
"Unless you have something important to say like offering a deal, don't waste my time."

The text wars were becoming less and less between us and in the end Robert, my lawyer, told me to stop and ignore him. So then Boaz tried the email approach:

Someone that had intentions of love, and is now confused and you turned me into a small-time criminal.

I appreciate the effort you have put in to tarnish my name to all the people I introduced you to. I feel used Lisa especially when you tell me you are independent. *I used my little savings to get you here. I am angry for that reason and disappointed of how you rubbish my name. So my going to prison or losing all will benefit you. I too lost moneywise. Whether I am man or not to you, it's not for you to judge.*

As normal even his emails were confusing. I'd had enough of this nonsense. So I emailed back:

It's not looking good for you. You can take my money but I have the truth on my side, if you do believe in your God he will be paying you a visit. I will always find some more money cos I am smart and I mix with good people. Not silly girls and crooks. If you're going to hate me just make sure you do it with full conviction. Let's see you go for the kill now Boaz, let me see what the man can do.

He wasn't getting inside my head again. I had a case file to prepare, ready for my day in court.

Thanks to hacking Boaz's email, I'd managed to get copies of some of the emails between Boaz and me that proved we were planning to get married. Along with our Skype chats where he said how much he loved me and missed me. All our plans, our hopes, our dreams. The land and the cattle we were going to buy. All there, in black and white.

Baby about having land and a upcountry place with cattle and if possible a huge farm it's my dream… it will take time but slowly I will get there. Slow but sure. I am happy I have a person that loves me, like I had always dreamed and that's a dream come true for me. I am happy I found you, you know.

It was hard to read; to think we were once like this. Reading my own words was just as painful. While staying in Texas with Randy I'd written:

I hope you are going to look after me when I get to Uganda cuz I will be scared. I have told Randy all about you and he is so happy for me. He can't wait to meet you. He already loves you and thinks u r cool for being a military man. He gave me a great big hug when I told him that you had asked me to marry you and he had big tears in his eyes.

I cried when I read his reply:

Of course I will look after you, I am not going to take my eyes off u baby.

I now had copies of the emails about my flights and Boaz's reply confirming he'd meet me at the airport. A copy of my e-ticket along with some of the shipping company emails. How could Boaz deny we were planning a life together when he'd written, *My wife Lisa will call you today or tomorrow about the pick-up arrangements.* I also had proof I'd paid for the shipping; an invoice clearly stamped – *Paid in cash by Morgan on 20th November 2011.* Along with emails between Boaz and the shipping company, giving pick-up details.

I even had a copy of the email Boaz sent asking what papers I needed to marry a Ugandan national. Here was a man in a hurry:

Sorry to bother you madam but I really need your help. I last visited your office in the previous month enquiring about civil marriage. My wife to be is a British National. She has only been here since 2nd May 2012 and we're so much interested to get married here in Uganda. The biggest predicament is the papers you advised me that she had to get. The letter of no impediment proving she had never got married before. Well we managed to apply for it online and we will have it soon. I really request please if you can, when we receive the letter could we possibly, through your help, cut short the dates of Notice which is supposed to be 20 days to minimum or quick as we can. Am requesting because of the need to stabilize and work our way through and advise if there will be further requirement apart from the mention so we are well set when the letter comes in. Waiting to hear from you.

I'd also managed to get a copy of the bank transfer of $69,000 US dollars from my Lebanon bank account. Reasons for transfer: *Moving to Uganda to get married.* Why would I do that if I didn't think we had a future together? Of course he was meant to move the money into our joint account. But that account never existed.

No wonder Boaz was trying to destroy it all. Here was proof he was a liar and a thief. No Judge in the land could ignore this.

Chapter Nine

Here Comes the Judge

After a pre-hearing with the Judge we finally got a date to start the actual trial.

We had to exchange evidence but when the day came Boaz's lawyer gave us nothing because he had nothing. It was two weeks later before we saw their defence. I was amazed by what I saw. Lies, lies and more lies.

The defendant upon arrival in Uganda went ahead to purchase his own household items which included a television set, washing machine and fridge. The plaintiff instructed the defendant to open up a bank account in his name, since she was not around for which her dues from her employers in Iraq would be transferred.

The defendant started noticing unbecoming conduct which included disappearances from home, heavy drinking with unknown people. The defendant shall contend that the money sent on his account belonging to the plaintiff was not for anything to do with preparation of any marriage but for her own personal benefits and as such any document acquired by the plaintiff with the sole intention of marriage was acquired falsely.

And Boaz had this letter with my signature, confirming that he had given me all my money back. And he had exchanged money to buy the furniture on 28th April 2012; just before I arrived in Uganda. I told Robert it wasn't true but I couldn't work out how Boaz had got my signature. Robert said not to worry about it. Delaying for so long was unprofessional and would go against them. He would bring it all up in court.

My case was straightforward.

The Plaintiff's claim is for breach of contract to marry, a refund of USD 69,431 and general damages. The plaintiff will contend that the company BA Financial Solutions belongs to both of them, the Defendant has completely excluded the Plaintiff from all transactions of the company.

Not long after her arrival in Uganda she was treated to a very bad reception by the Defendant who turned rude against the Plaintiff. The Defendant continued to be very rude to the Plaintiff and telling her that he will never marry her.

There it was in black and white. I liked the use of the word rude though Boaz was a lot more than that.

I'd waited months for my day in court. The case was being heard in the Judge's chambers rather than a courtroom. I felt numb when I saw Boaz. There was this silence in my head and I couldn't quite understand why he would choose money over love. I was sat on the left and Boaz was on the right, with our lawyers in the middle. We were like two bookends. Realising this was a sensitive case; the Judge had decided to hold the hearings in his chambers to keep the press out. There are few restrictions on the press in Uganda and they love a bit of scandal. And I guess I was becoming noticed; any case involving a foreigner was big news.

To make sure the sessions were kept private, the door was shut and the Judge's bodyguard was posted outside. Most Judges in Uganda have bodyguards or some sort of security. Not only to protect them but to stop anyone from trying to bribe them. I'd always been in fear of Boaz getting to the Judge like he'd got to that Susan. I had never been in front of a Judge before or even had a speeding ticket. But I could see that Justice Benjamin Kabiito was a good Judge. He was younger than I'd expected; probably late 40's, maybe 50 and well dressed in an immaculate suit. He was strict and did everything by the book. And he made it clear that he wasn't going to stand for any nonsense. All he was interested in was the facts. There was also a secretary and three law students who were just observing.

The trial was a slow process and I noticed one of the students had fallen asleep on the sofa, but no one seemed to care.

After a break there would be me, Boaz and our lawyers sat together in a waiting room, before the hearing began again. Boaz would never speak to me. But he would make sure there was plenty of eye contact. Once he came and stood next to me. It was quite bizarre.

"Lisa, why are you doing this to me?" I didn't reply. His lawyer dragged him away. He made me nervous yet he also made me feel like I'd somehow misjudged him. Had I missed something? Was it me? Am I the bad one? I was finding it hard to focus on reality. I allowed my heart to be on display and started to cry; his lawyer noticed.

"Oh my God, she's crying." I cried during the entire case.

I remember one time we were sat round a large table in the Judge's chambers when I dropped my pen on the floor. As I leant forward to pick it up our eyes met. Boaz had such beautiful black eyes. I felt all the memories of being in love with this man racing around my head. It was like a weird kind of *Stockholm Syndrome*, but captured by my own lover. The excitement; the falling out, the making-up, the hurt, even the bruises. My head was spinning like a washing machine. Boaz was staring at me. But this time the stare was one of unhappiness and sadness. I quickly picked up my pen and sat up straight but I couldn't hide the tears running down my face. I think I broke down in tears every day in court. How could Boaz put me through this? Force me to take him to court. We could have sorted all this out between us instead of ending up before a Judge. Couldn't we? All I wanted was my money even just some of it; if I can't have that at least let me leave with some dignity.

I hated every second of being in court. I felt so sad and lonely but I had to go forward. I'd got nowhere with the criminal case so Robert and I were ready to do battle. We had prepared our civil case well and logged everything in chronological order; spending hours rehearsing it all in Robert's office.

The court case was a slow process as everything had to be written down by hand. My lawyer would go through my file and ask questions and I would answer. Then he'd present a piece of evidence to the Judge. We had court once a week, or every two weeks. It was painfully slow and an emotional roller coaster. One of the worst moments was when Robert described my arrival in Uganda.

"So the defendant picked you up from the airport?"
"Yes, well no."

Everyone looked at me including the Judge.

"You mean he didn't pick you up?" asked the Judge.
"I mean he wasn't there."
The Judge looked confused. "Alright, Miss Morgan. I would like to hear more about this."
"When I arrived at the airport he wasn't there. I was waiting an hour or more by the taxi rank. But he wasn't there."
"So let me get this right. You have shipped everything to Uganda. You have moved from one country to another, left your job. You got off an international flight, having arrived in another continent, and there was no one to collect you at the airport?"
"Yes, correct."
"But you called him."
"I left my phone in Lebanon so I called him from Ethiopia."
"How could you call him if you didn't have your phone?"
"My friend Rita gave me his number as I had been using her phone and I wrote it on the inside of my ticket. I used someone else's phone when I changed planes in Ethiopia but he never answered."

The Judge wasn't happy. "Why hasn't this been submitted in evidence? This is proof she left her phone and was trying to make contact so we have a sequence of communication all the way through. Why aren't you helping your client?"

Now it dawned on me. Was Boaz actually planning to leave me at the airport? Surely not. But I was beginning to realise that the timescale was all wrong. When Boaz had said he was going to be twenty minutes, and was on his way, I don't think he was on his way. I don't think he had even left the apartment. Would he really have left me stranded at the airport?

I hadn't realised how important this piece of evidence was but the Judge did. He was quite sharp. He wasn't pleased and looked at Boaz and his lawyer and then started writing. He wrote everything down. The Judge became very concerned about the speed of the case and for my survival in this country; he even cancelled some of his holiday, to speed up the whole process.

In between the court days I would meet up with Cecilia at her golf club and have lunch. She'd ask me how things were going.

"Yes, things are going well since he moved out. It's better for me but it's a bit weird. I still feel a connection with him."

"Yes, for sure you will," said Cecilia.

"I forgot to tell you that before he left he turned up one day in a terrible state; he had marks on his neck and chest. I could see blood seeping through his shirt."

"Oh my God." Cecilia was horrified. "Tell me more."

"Well, I saw the blood and I told him to take the shirt off. He had cuts on the back of his neck and on his chest. He was weak and I was a bit worried. He said a cat scratched him but it was a lie."

"Of course it was. So what did you do next?"

"I ran a hot bath and told him to get in it. Then I told him to get in bed and he stayed there for three whole days. He was very sick. He didn't move and never spoke; I had to look after him. I'm not without heart Cecilia."

Cecilia looked scared. "Lisa, he has been to a witch doctor and sold himself to the Devil."

I laughed. "But witch doctors aren't real. Are they? Please Cecilia, you're scaring me."

"I think Boaz was selling his soul to the Devil," said Cecilia. "He's trying to protect himself from harm and get rid of his demons." Cecilia sat shaking her head. "From the church to the Devil. Lisa, it's too late to help him now."

I didn't like this conversation. I didn't know anything about this black magic stuff and witchcraft. I didn't believe such things but Cecilia knew something definitely wasn't right.

Boaz was forever calling or texting me. I told Robert I wasn't going to reply anymore but sometimes I gave in. All he wanted to know was where I was and what I was doing. I think it was some kind of control thing. He even wished me good luck before my court case. All this was starting to freak me out.

Robert said we need to hurry up and get through the deceit, the other women and get to the money stuff. But all the time I kept thinking how on earth was Boaz able to prove he had bought the furniture. It bugged me but he had this piece of evidence. The receipt from the Bank of Uganda clearly saying he'd exchanged money at the Forex Bureau. And it had happened before I arrived in the country. But to me it was impossible.

I'd been introduced to a Police Officer called Ochen. He was going to help me with further investigations. I was convinced I was missing something. I hoped that if I found this 'something' during the court case, Ochen could be a witness and present it in court. Ochen's English was perfect and he was on the ball. Joshua had helped me as much as he could and was still chasing the Department of Public Prosecutions report. But I didn't want Susan making things any harder for him, so I tried not to involve him anymore.

Ochen had to get approval from his Commander before he could help me.

"This girl Lisa is from England and she has been robbed by this Ugandan. He has taken all her money. It is a bad situation. I am going to assist her with further investigations." Fortunately, the Commander was fine about it.

I had a case number so was able to get a court order to access Boaz's phone records. Ochen had a code he could use to identify mobile numbers, and the registered owner. I never mentioned this Christine. I wanted to test him to see if this code really worked. We met up and Ochen had a copy of Boaz's phone records. I highlighted the numbers for him to check. These were numbers Boaz had called regularly. There was one number that stood out. He had called it one hundred and fifty times in one month alone. Ochen checked it out.

"It belongs to a girl called Christine."

I knew it; here was more proof of his lies. Now I could link them altogether. How was that little rat going to get out of that? I was hurt all over again but the pain had started to feel normal.

These records even showed the areas he had made the calls from. Now I knew he had been to Christine's house, where the car had been and where Boaz was staying during the night. Ochen was great. I really loved this guy. He was in his early 30's and divorced with two girls. He was a worker, full of energy, knew his job and best of all, he was on my side.

I asked Ochen to look into Rebecca, Boaz's sister. She worked in a bank in town so maybe she was in on it. Boaz had an account there that I didn't know about until recently so Ochen paid her a visit. Boaz's sister was standing behind the bank teller when Ochen asked if Boaz had a bank account there.

"Yes he does. Rebecca, isn't that your brother he's talking about?"
"Yes, it is. What do you want with him?"
"Oh, we are just investigating a case."
"My brother has not done anything wrong. Can I take your number and I will get him to call you?"
"No, no that won't be necessary."

But somehow his sister called and told Ochen to leave her brother alone. And then Boaz calls. How they got the number is a mystery.

Boaz thought they should meet up. "We should have a meeting. I am quite open to discussion."

Boaz was crafty. I wasn't sure if it was a good idea for Ochen to meet up with Boaz but he disagreed.

"Do not worry. It will put pressure on him. Play him at his own game and if he panics, he will make a mistake."

Clever but I insisted he didn't meet with both of them. I couldn't afford for anything to go wrong.

After Ochen made the connection with Rebecca, Ochen's Commander asked if he knew why this Susan from CID was calling. She wanted to know if he was helping me with my case. Ochen wasn't sure why she was calling but I knew why. She'd never forgiven me for complaining about her. Susan was going to make things difficult for me. The Commander called her back but she never answered. She'd found out all she needed to know; Ochen was helping me with my investigations and she didn't like it.

We were making progress but Boaz put a spanner in the works and told the Judge he wasn't available for the next three weeks. The Judge had to honour it but I wasn't happy. This was a blow to me but at least I had friends who were still helping me out financially. It took some of the pressure off.

Robert wanted to use the time to go over the evidence the defence had presented.

"Morgan, are you sure you didn't sign any of these papers saying he gave you your money back?"
"Yes, I am sure. But remember he had access to my evidence thanks to that Susan. My signature was everywhere."

The first document was a statement in Boaz's handwriting and signed by me:

Acknowledgement
I Morgan Lisa Ann acknowledge receipt of $20,000 USD from Boaz Asingwire. However, $10,300 USD was given back to him as contribution to purchasing the car. And I also acknowledge receiving some money equivalent to $34,300 on 6th July 2012. The said above is correct to the best of my knowledge.

He must be joking. How could anyone believe this? I had never seen this piece of paper before in my life yet I could see it was my signature. Robert gave me some great advice.

"Right Morgan, all you have to say is, 'No, that is not my signature. But it looks like my signature.' Morgan, they have to prove it, not you. They will have to get a handwriting expert but it will take time. They are trying to break you. The problem is that they have left you with nothing to negotiate with. Boaz wants it all and if this letter sticks with the Judge, you're finished."

Oh lord, Robert was smart and right.

"Remember Morgan, they just have to prove it's your signature. If we could get something, just one thing, we can close him down."

It was beginning to dawn on me that Boaz had planned this deceit all along. All he needed was a bent lawyer to help him.

That receipt was still bugging me. Boaz's lawyer had included it in his defence but he hadn't yet presented it in court. I wasn't happy about it but I felt like there was nothing I could do. This receipt seemed to show that Boaz had exchanged several thousand US dollars' days before I arrived in Uganda. It was proof that Boaz had paid for all the furniture etc. It also supported Boaz's claim that I was his guest and he'd never asked me to marry him. It was dated and stamped and looked very official but it was wrong. So wrong. I told Robert something wasn't right. It was some sort of fake.

I couldn't sleep that night; I was up and down. I felt like I was hallucinating; going a bit crazy. My head was spinning. Was Boaz right about the dates? Had I got it wrong? No, no, he was lying.

After little sleep I woke up with a plan of action. I was the one who had to do something. That morning I headed for the Bank of Uganda. I was going to get some answers. I had no idea how this was going to turn out but it was better than doing nothing. In Uganda every time you try to do something you meet a brick wall. And another brick wall. And another. The frustration will kill you.

I was on a mission and steaming down the streets of Kampala when I ran into Joshua, my man from CID.

"Sorry, can't stop. I have something very important to do. Will call you."

I arrived at the Bank of Uganda and told them I had a bit of a problem and showed them the copy of the receipt.

I made up a story as I didn't want anyone to know what I was up to. "My friends came to visit me and they've left something in this bureau place. They asked me to check if it is still there but I'm unable to read the stamp. Can you tell me which Forex Bureau this is?"

The clerk was very helpful. "I know exactly where it is. I am going that way myself so I will take you there."

Now Kampala is a very busy city and crossing the roads can be a killer so I held on to this man from the bank for dear life. As I got near to the bureau I said I had to do a bit of shopping first, knowing he wouldn't hang around. So he directed me the rest of the way and I thanked him.

At the bureau I asked to see the Manager. I couldn't let them see how much I was shaking inside, I had to stay calm. I felt like a private eye in a TV detective drama. The Manager appeared.

"Hello," I said with a smile. "This receipt, is it from here?"
"Yes," he replied.
"Good because this man stole my money."
He was taken aback. "Oh, no."
"I just want to know if this serial number matches a particular date and time." "Yes, yes I understand. Come to the office please and I will help you."

He sat me down and studied the receipt then he checked the computer. It wasn't on the system. He looked puzzled. Not everywhere in Uganda is computerized. Even back in CID, I wasn't sure if they even knew how to turn the computer on. So the Manager then disappeared and came back carrying a large, old-fashioned ledger and started flicking through it. I didn't speak. I was too nervous to say anything.

The Manager stopped at a page and started looking through this huge log of numbers, referring to transactions on that particular date. There were masses of them but of course I'm asking him to check back to over a year ago. But being an auditor it didn't take him long to find the serial number.

I held my breath as he started to speak.

"This is it; this is the one. But it never happened on this day."
 "What?" I could barely speak.
"No, this transaction was not done on the 28th of April 2012. It was done on the 8th of May 2012. On the original receipt, which I have, it is different. Some information is missing while on yours it is filled in."

Son of a bitch! I wanted to kiss the man.
"So this is good news?" I said.
"Well, that depends what side you're on. Are you taking him to court?"
"Yes sir."
 "Well, you go get your Police Officer and I will speak to our lawyer."

Boaz had left details off the receipt like the date and passport number. According to the rules and law of the Bank of Uganda, these are details you are supposed to fill in if it's a transaction over $5,000 US dollars. He had kept the receipt for over a year and filled in the details to make out I wasn't even in the country when the money was exchanged.

The Manager continued to explain. "You see the details here, on the original receipt, they are missing. But on his copy those details, including the date, have been filled in. And I know this for sure as this is the master copy and the serial numbers have to run in order."

Boaz had probably bribed the bank teller who, conveniently, no longer worked there to leave bits of the receipt blank. Here was proof that Boaz had exchanged the money after I arrived in Uganda; not before. It was my money not his that paid for the furniture, the TV; everything I bought for the apartment. As I left the bureau I was like a woman on fire. This piece of evidence was crucial and it was going to win my case

I called Ochen. I told him what I had found and he made his way to see the Manager. This was the letter that was written by the lawyer representing the Forex Bureau.

20th July 2013
Your Worship
We act for and on behalf of Lloyds Forex Bureau Ltd hereinafter referred to as our clients and reference is made to your order to inspect and take documents/copies of entries addressed to them.

Our clients have cross checked and found that the said transaction was made on the 8th May 2012 under receipt No 0282176 or US $5,500 equivalent of Ug Shs 13,530.000. The said receipt was between receipt No 0282175 and 0282177 (copies attached). Our clients are therefore not liable for any eventuality that may occur as the records are clear as stated above.

I met Ochen later at the *Khyber Pass* in Kampala to discuss our next move. Ochen would now have to apply to the court; as my witness he would have to present this evidence in court. For once something was going my way.

"This is great Lisa. This proves he committed fraud and there is no way on earth he can get out of it. The Judge will see him for what he really is."

Yeah it was great but I was mortified. Boaz had demoralized me as a woman, exchanged my love for my money. Yet my heart refused to switch off.

I still had to be careful around Kampala. I am quite easy to spot and had to make sure no one saw me or saw me with Ochen. Boaz had little spies everywhere. I went through everything with Ochen and couldn't wait for the date when he would come to court and present this evidence.

"Are you okay? You are going to be there aren't you?"
"Don't worry, I won't let you down."
"Okay, see you in court on Monday at 9.00am. Don't have an accident on the way home. Ha Ha."

Then I went to see Robert. "I have something."
He was with a client, so I waited.
"Morgan, what have you got?"
"You know that one thing we needed? Well you are not going to believe it."

And I showed him a copy of the lawyer's letter from the Forex Bureau.

"Damn Morgan. This is totally incriminating. The story is different now."
"Why's that?"
"Well, this is a criminal matter. Boaz has got himself into a lot of trouble."

Robert agreed that Boaz had probably set me up from the beginning. Yeah it's not a great feeling but what can I do? I will never really know if he planned it from the moment we met in Iraq or changed when he arrived back in Uganda. But none of that really mattered now.

Ochen organised the court summons:

22nd July 2012
To: Ochen Kelly

WHEREAS your attendance is required to give evidence in the above suit you are hereby required (personally) to appear before this Court on the 23rd day of July 2013 at 9.00AM. The Plaintiff shall meet your travelling and subsistence for the day. If you fail to comply with this order without lawful excuse, you will be subjected to the consequences of non-attendance laid down in the rules 12 of Order XIV of the CIVIL PROCEDURE RULES.

It was all systems go.

Chapter Ten

Tragedy

In between waiting for court dates I secretly met up with his uncle, who told me some home truths. Mugisha was genuinely concerned about me. He repeatedly told me to leave the country and make a new life. He was a good, decent man and still served in the Military.

"Do you remember when Boaz was in the army and this happened?" I asked.
He stopped me in my tracks. "Lisa that was not Boaz, that was me."
"But he was in the army wasn't he?"
"No, Lisa, Boaz was never in the army. Never."

More lies. I was astonished. "What about the Pygmy language? He said he'd learnt it when he was based in the Congo."
"I don't know," replied Mugisha. "Boaz is very smart; no one else can speak this language in our family, only him."

I remember we used to have a calendar in the apartment and Boaz had written on one day in June, '*Mugisha Hearing.*' He said his uncle needed help and might even go to jail and asked for money in case he had to pay bail.

"My uncle has got into a lot of trouble and I am going to help him."
"What sort of trouble?"
"There was a weapon used in a killing and now it's gone missing. It was in my uncle's custody."

Of course, I believed him. Boaz was away all that day, apparently in court. Now it appears to be a total fabrication. His uncle told me the case had nothing to do with Boaz or him. It was a story he'd told him about someone he knew in the army. The reason Boaz had lied was because he had to be somewhere for the whole day so it was a good excuse and, of course, to take more money. Is there any truth with this stupid boy?

And even worse, his Father hadn't been in the army either. And he hadn't died of a gunshot wound; he'd died of Aids. Another outrageous lie but I think Boaz was probably more ashamed or embarrassed by the cause of his Father's death.

Well none of that now mattered. It was Boaz's life and clearly I am no longer part of it. However, as hard as it was for me, the earth still revolved and wasn't going to wait for me to wipe away yet another tear. I had to find the strength but my health was suffering.

I was having some difficulties with my eyesight. Everything was getting blurry and I think it was due to the amount of stress I was under. It didn't help that I was without a TV and I was watching movies on a ten-inch computer screen. It was straining my eyes. So on my next trip to the *Lugogo* shopping mall I saw a shop that did free eye testing. I liked the shopping mall; it was only a twenty minute boda-boda ride away and had everything I needed; beauty shops, food shops. It was also home to the *Good African* coffee shop where I'd met Hannah for the first time.

I'd picked up my glasses the next day and was sat at my computer desk in Boaz's old bedroom. I remember the date; it was 3rd July 2013. While I was looking at the screen my eyes suddenly felt like they were jumping up and down very quickly. Oh no, these glasses are no good. But then my desk chair rolled backwards on its wheels to the middle of the room. What the hell was going on? It took me about fifteen seconds to realise we were having an earthquake. It wasn't much of an earthquake at first, but it progressed and got gradually worse. I'd say it lasted about two minutes but seems like a lifetime. It was so intense that my wardrobe doors shook violently and broke off the hinges.

I didn't know what to do. I could hear Charlotte next door screaming which made me laugh nervously. I was gripping tightly to my chair as the earth shook around me. I kept thinking this isn't going to do my bloody eyes any good. I can't focus! As the shaking intensified, I tried to run to the doorway but the floor was so uneven it threw me off balance and I ended up on my knees. But I finally managed to get underneath the door frame. It was probably the best thing to do as it felt like the safest place to be if the house fell down.

I was amazed by this earthquake. I have never in my life been that close to the fury of Mother Nature.

Another earthquake came later in the night but I was already in bed. I laid there in silence, holding my breath and wondering if the roof was going to cave in on me or I was going to end up wrapped around banana tree.

The next day I went down to Jackie's shop. Everyone had gathered together and was sharing their stories of that night's earthquake; where we were, what we were doing, how close we'd come to death. We were laughing and joking with one of the boda-boda guys. He told us about his pots and pans falling off the shelves and hitting him on the head while he was sleeping. The tiles had come off an old lady's house so we all helped to fix it. Apparently it was quite a large earthquake; around 5.7 in magnitude. And had originated from Lake Albert, which was quite a distance from us; around 230 kilometres away.

I had survived an earthquake. Now I had to survive a court case. I had proof over and over again of Boaz's lies and the day had arrived when he was going to be found out. Ochen was my star witness and he was going to present my new evidence. But 9 o'clock came and Ochen was nowhere to be seen. We took a break and I called him but his phone was switched off. Where was he? I started to panic. This evidence was key to my case. It proved Boaz was a liar and had produced fake evidence. I turned to my lawyer.

"Robert he should have been here by now. I saw him the other day and he said he'd be here at 9.00 am. I don't understand. He's never late."

I called his mobile over and over again but it was switched off. Oh my God, what if he's been in an accident? What if someone had tried to hurt him? I knew that Susan was sniffing around my case. She'd already tried to intimidate Ochen. No, surely she wouldn't have done anything to him, would she?

I was worried sick. Luckily we didn't have time for Ochen's witness statement and the Judge wanted to end the session for the day so we finished at 1 pm. For once, the abrupt ending of the court session couldn't have come at a better time; *TIA - This is Africa.*

I headed for Ochen's police station I had to find out where he was. He wasn't there and I asked his Commander if he knew where he was. His Commander was busy, busy fixing other people's problems. And he was familiar with those who had been caught out by the temptations of the honey pot. I introduced myself.

"You might not know who I am but my name is Lisa Morgan."
"I do; you are the Muzungu who married the Ugandan."
"I am not married to this man. Your Officer, Ochen, has been working with me and he has disappeared. And I am very concerned."

I told him about this Susan and how she had messed up everything; leaving all my evidence on the backseat of a car. I had this horrible feeling that she might have had something to do with Ochen's disappearance. She was not to be trusted. The Commander didn't like to comment too much but he wasn't surprised. And he was aware of my story; everyone was. He apologised and told me not to worry. "I will organise a search party."

Everyone was out looking for this guy. If something had happened to Ochen, because of my case, I would never forgive myself. I was told to wait there so I sat on a large rocking chair on a wooden platform that led up to the Commander's office. It was like something out of the *OK Corral* and I was just waiting for the cowboys and Indians to turn up. From here I could see the moment Ochen came back; if he came back. So where was he? Everyone agreed this was most unlike him. Ochen was never late and he always answered his phone. He was reliable and trustworthy. I didn't know what to do so I decided to wait. He was bound to turn up here.

I'd been sitting there for hours watching the police and thieves coming and going; the endless arguments the blaming, the finger pointing. But there was no sign of my Officer. I waited and waited and waited and I smoked and smoked. The police changed shifts and new ones came on duty. It was dark by now but I was still sitting there; swinging my legs and puffing away.

I got chatting to some of the Officers who regularly checked to see if I was okay.

"We are off for our dinner now but we will come back to see how you are."

One of the officers suggested I sit in a Police car to keep warm and away from the mosquitoes. We were talking about cars when Ochen walked up.

One of the Officers was curious. "Hello, where have you been? This Muzungu girl has been waiting for you."

"Lisa, I am so sorry I let you down."

"Are you alright?" I was really worried about you."

"I need to speak to my Commander. Can you wait here?"

I could see how upset he was. He walked upstairs and disappeared into the Commander's office. When he came out he said his Commander wanted to speak to me. I had a bad feeling about all this.

The Commander explained that Susan had asked Ochen to come to her office at 10.30 that morning to discuss my case. She should have gone through the chain of command but had gone direct which didn't look good. But as she was the higher rank she could make Ochen's life difficult.

"Lisa, I realise everybody has let you down. This Officer really wants to help you but it is his choice. I cannot force him to help you."

"I am just trying to get my money back. Please help me. Please, I beg you." And I burst into tears.

The Commander reached out and held my hand. I was so close now. I had the evidence that would prove Boaz stole my money, but without Ochen's help I couldn't present it in court. It was over. I went outside to see my Officer.

Ochen explained he'd gone to see his Father to speak to him, instead of meeting up with this Susan. His Father was a very wise man and he had spent the day talking to him about my case.

"My Father said you joined the police service to put bad people away and to serve your country. You have to follow what you think is right. What is in your heart? It is your choice. But Lisa you know 'things' happen here and I have two children."

He was emotional and had a tear in his eye. I had such a bond with this Officer it upset me to see him like this. I gave him a big hug and told him not to worry about it; I will find a way. But as I was about to say my goodbyes he changed his mind.

"No, I can't, I can't give up on you, I am going to help you Lisa. I joined this Police force to help people; I know it's corrupt but we're not all the same. I have a duty to help you and that's what I'm going to do. We will do this together."

Oh the relief. I hugged him so hard I nearly squeezed the life out of him.

"Thank you, thank you. I don't know how to repay you. I don't have anything to give you. But thank you."
"Lisa we are going to nail this Boaz. I must go and tell my Commander of my decision."

The Commander was impressed by Ochen's bravery and told him to carry on the good work. But be careful. I never really got to the bottom of why this Susan was so interested in my case. I can't prove it but a lot of people said Boaz bribed her. Someone told me she had taken sides before in other cases. But I believe what goes around comes around and I have the truth on my side.

But in the end Ochen never presented any evidence. We only had a few more court sessions to go and were days away from getting the verdict. I was very happy and had started packing and organising my things, ready to leave the country. But then just before we were due back in court I got a call from Mr Masana, who was the Deputy Director of CID. He asked if I could attend a meeting the next morning; Boaz would be present. I was surprised and notified Robert. He told me to go and update him later.

When I arrived at CID Headquarters I saw Boaz, who was on the phone as usual. We would have to wait over an hour before we would get to see Mr Masana. Boaz spotted me and came closer.

We both ended up sitting on the wall and our eyes met. I hadn't seen him for at least three weeks nor spoken to him as I never answered his calls. The text wars had ended and I no longer answered his emails.

Finally, we were summoned to Mr Masana's office. Boaz was sat one end of the sofa and I was sat at the other. There was another Officer in the room. It was the same Officer who had wanted me to come in and make a statement about hacking Boaz's emails. I was worried. Mr Masana started to explain that the Department of Public Prosecution's report was in and its findings were final. They were closing the case and gave us both a copy. Then he said he wanted the car moved.

I looked at the date; it was April 2013 and it was now 6th August 2013. You had to be kidding me. This report had been withheld from me and after I read it I could see why. It was inconclusive and it was obvious they wanted to put the case to bed.

18th April 2013
Obtaining Money by False Pretences – Uganda versus Asingwire Boaz
The complainant (Lisa Morgan) met with one Asingwire Boaz, a Ugandan while both were working in Iraq. They fell in love and agreed to get married. Consequently, Lisa Morgan decided to transfer all her personal belongings including money to Uganda with the hope of officially getting married to Boaz. But within months they developed misunderstandings that resulted into quarrels, fights and disagreements. These bred malicious damage and assault case which were reported to various police stations and police posts. Due to the fights and mistrusts between the two, Lisa Morgan demanded for the accountability of the money deposited on the suspect's account.

In the circumstances we find that the charges of obtaining money by false pretence cannot be successfully sustained against the suspect. The money was wilfully deposited on the suspect's bank account. The complainant does not dispute that part of the money was withdrawn and spent with her consent.

Therefore, could not have been done under false pretence of marriage. Conclusion is to close and put away the case file as evidence was insufficient to sustain the charge. The complainant was advised to seek for civil remedy.

As far as they were concerned the money transfers proved I'd handed the money over willingly. And suggested I might get further with a civil case! Thanks for nothing. But there was some good news.

The charges are assault and domestic violence against the suspect Asingwire Boaz. The allegations are that on 20/10/2012 the two had a fight. The suspect hit the complainant to the extent that she was taken to hospital. Accordingly, there is sufficient evidence to sustain the charges of assault and domestic violence against the suspect. The charges are hereby sanctioned.

The report also calculated the funds that had been paid towards the car, the house and household items and an amount that was 'handed back to me.' Well, that would explain the letter Boaz had submitted as evidence in the civil case; the letter I had supposedly signed. Somehow the DPP seemed to know more about my money and its whereabouts than I did. I had never got any updates from Susan before my evidence was submitted to the DPP. And the delay to seeing the report was significant as it meant I couldn't act on or dispute the findings. But none of this really mattered anymore. I had an ace up my sleeve with the Forex Bureau evidence. Let's see Boaz explain that one.

The Deputy wanted the car to be moved so I told him I would speak to my lawyer and get it moved to the Civil Court's compound. Boaz piped up that it wasn't my decision. I told him, "Shut your face," and quietly added, "that car will be the death of you." I continued to speak and told the Deputy I needed a few days to organise the paperwork.
It was about time I had the upper hand. I told Robert what had happened and he immediately drafted a letter to the civil court to move the car.

When I got home I had a nice hot shower and washed the dust out of my hair. I was feeling good and excited. With only days to go I felt finally free from all this nonsense.

While in the shower I missed a call from Boaz. Oh no, what does he want now? I didn't want to hear what he had to say so I ignored him. But the calls didn't stop. Maybe I should answer. It could be something serious. He might be ringing to tell me his grandmother, who had cancer, had died. I had seen him earlier that day in the Deputy's office; maybe he missed me? Ha, I doubt that. Okay, it was 6th of August, two years exactly since he asked me to marry him. Maybe he had come over all sentimental. I nervously answered the sixth call.

"Why didn't you answer your phone?"
"Well I'm answering now. What do you want?"
"Nothing."
"Then why are you calling me?"
"I just wanted to hear your voice"

I could almost hear him smile and for a brief moment I was captivated by him all over again.

"Really?" I laughed, "It's nearly midnight."
"Yes I know." For a moment he was silent.
"Well, I'm coming over to..."
"What? Hello, hello?"

The signal was lost. I lay on my bed with a towel still wrapped around my head and the light off. I was unsure what he meant or what he really wanted but I decided not to ring back and drifted off to sleep with the phone in my hand.

I struggled to sleep. Sometimes I suffer from restless leg syndrome and tonight I was kicking badly. I kept tossing and turning and was trying to get back to sleep when I heard the phone ring. It was about 1.30 am. It must be him calling me back. I answered and was surprised to hear a woman's voice.

"Is that Lisa?"
"Yes."

"It's Rebecca, Boaz's sister. I was just wondering if Boaz was with you."
"No." Why on earth would she think he would be with me?
"It's just he's normally back by now."
"Have you tried calling him?"
"His phone is off. Have you seen him?"
"No, I haven't but he called earlier. Maybe his battery's died. Don't worry about it. I am sure he will be back."

He might be a bastard but I didn't want anything to happen to him. He'd probably gone partying. I don't know. I never knew what he got up to. I lay back down and tried to sleep.

Thirty minutes later Rebecca called again. She was hysterical. "Boaz is dead, Boaz is dead."
I was still half asleep. "Is this a damn joke?" But she was screaming down the phone. "Hang on. Calm down. Who told you he was dead?"
She was struggling to get her words out. "I called his phone and this man answered. He had Boaz's phone. He works in the mortuary at Mulago hospital. He said he was dead."
Oh no, you're kidding me. "Hold on, hold on. Okay. Listen. I am going to call you back. I need to do something. Have you got someone with you?"
"My brother Benjamin is coming."
"Will you be okay?" But I couldn't get anything more out of her. I didn't know if I believed her. So I called Boaz's phone. An unfamiliar voice answered.

"Hello, this is the phone of Boaz."
"Yes hello. Who are you?"
"This is Joseph from Mulago Hospital. Are you the wife?"
"Well I'm Lisa."
"Lisa I work in the mortuary. I am very sorry but Boaz is dead. He died instantly, he didn't feel any pain. He was in a car accident. There was nothing anyone could have done."

I couldn't make sense of these words and my brain went into overload. I had to be sure he was talking about Boaz.

115

"I don't get it, it can't be him, he doesn't have a car."
"Yes he was the driver and there was another, but he's not dead. I don't know much about what's happened to him."
"Can you do something; can you check his pockets and find some ID? He has three names."

Boaz didn't have a wallet as he'd lost it. Joseph found some papers and read out a name – Boaz…
Slowly I answered. "Okay. That's his name."
Still I wasn't convinced.

I remember trembling at that point. I was sat on the side of the bed feeling cold and numb. Boaz must have saved my number under wife in his phone.
"You should come down here and see him," said Joseph.
"Yes, yes I will come, I will come down now."
"I spoke to his auntie but she is in the village. And his sister. I have just been going through his phone but you are the first to call in."
"Okay, okay, I will come now."

I was shaking by now and praying it wasn't him. I called Bernard who was a boda-boda guy who lived down Nabe Road, next to Jackie's. I knew he would be awake and answer the phone.

"Sorry Bernard I need you to take me to the Hospital."
"Are you sick, I do not know if I have any fuel in my bike? But I will check."

Bernard arrived at my gate at two in the morning. I told him someone had said Boaz was dead and was at Mulago Hospital, but I was unsure if it was him. It was pouring with rain but there wasn't much traffic. All the petrol stations were closed but luckily there was just enough petrol to get to the hospital. I was wearing a rain jacket and a baseball hat. I was holding on to Bernard, telling him not to go too fast. I was nervous riding in the rain.

It's a thirty-minute drive to the hospital. Bernard said he'd wait for me but I told him to go and I'd call him.

Bernard asked the security guard where I should go and he directed me to the lady behind a desk. At this point I was still unsure if it was really him. I said I'd been told my husband, boyfriend was dead. I didn't know what I should call him. I asked if she could point me in the direction of the mortuary. She gave me directions but they were complicated

"Turn around, go straight ahead; when you get to the third door you will see a spiral staircase that leads downstairs. Turn right at the bottom and then turn left."

How the hell am I supposed to remember all that? I asked if anyone could come with me but she said she was sorry but she was all alone and couldn't leave the desk.

I tried to follow her directions and managed to get to the lower floors. The smell of disinfectant was getting stronger and stronger. When I reached the bottom I pushed open a door which led to a long corridor. I stood there for a minute and stared down this long tunnel. My legs wouldn't move; all I could hear was the loud noise of the rain and the lights flickering. I felt sick and dizzy. I couldn't see anyone so I called Joseph, the mortuary attendant, to let him know I was here. He appeared at the end of the corridor. Slowly I found the strength and started walking towards him.

On my right was what looked like wooden stable doors. I almost didn't want to reach the end because when I did, I would know for sure whether Boaz was dead or alive. I'd noticed that behind these stable doors were pink and blue files tied up in bundles and stacked really high. Every one of those files represented a dead soul. As I walked past it was almost as if I could hear the dead whispering and chattering. I was so scared I nearly froze but I kept my eyes focused on Joseph the entire time. I felt as if I was walking in slow motion.

As I walked I remembered how scared I'd been of the dark as a child. The walk along the landing to my bedroom always seemed so long and so so scary. This walk felt exactly the same. My heart was pounding.

Joseph was wearing a rubber-like pinafore. He was friendly and sympathetic.

"I am very sorry for your loss."

His phone rang and he said Lisa is here and passed me the phone.

"Hello Lisa this is the aunty to Boaz."
"Oh hello." I didn't know her but all his family seemed to know me.
"Lisa, I am so sorry." At that moment I didn't really want to speak to her. But it was looking more and more likely that Boaz really was dead. I handed the phone back to Joseph and tried to keep myself together.
I am petrified of the dead and wasn't sure if I could do this. I'd seen my mum after she died. She was lying on the bed at home and my sister made me go and see her. But I never wanted to see my brother; that would have tipped me over board for sure. Joseph asked if I was ready.

Now I had to be strong. I was okay. No I wasn't okay. Wait, wait. I need a minute. I could hear my brother's voice. "If you are ever in a situation you are unfamiliar with, breathe it, smell it, open your eyes." Okay, I can do this now. I told Joseph I was scared of the dead. He said not to worry; he'd heard that before; I wasn't the first person to feel that way.

"Wait, is he a mess, you know, like blood and stuff?"
"No, no he is not. Now come."

I asked him to hold my hand and he gently led me through the plastic doors, through another set of doors and into a large room. And out of the corner of my eye I could see a body.

Chapter Eleven

Freak Accident

I remember that body so well. It was an old man with a thin face and no shoes. He wasn't covered up. He was wearing a thick woollen jumper; it almost looked like he had a sheep lying on top of him. I could hear my brother's voice telling me to keep my eyes open; "Get yourself in the zone." Then I saw another body. It was a huge man and he was lying on a table quite high up. At least he had a sheet over him. Joseph was still holding my hand but I was struggling. Here I was surrounded by things I wasn't used to. But TIA – this is *Africa*. Then we turned the corner.

All I could see were a pair of legs sticking out. Although this body wasn't covered up, I couldn't see the head as another body was in the way. There were bodies everywhere. But the jeans and a boot looked familiar. I took a deep breath. My life was about to change in five seconds flat. I needed to be ready. I could feel my brother standing next to me; giving me strength. I recognised the boot; one was missing. The boot was one of a nice pair of tan ankle boots, elasticated at the side. He was dressed in blue jeans and the brown pin striped shirt he had been wearing the last time I saw him. It was Boaz lying there.

I approached the table and stared at his lifeless body.
His lovely big, black eyes were slightly open. Joseph let go of my hand.
"Please don't go, don't leave me. Promise you won't leave me."
"I promise."
He wandered to the back of the room to give me some time alone.

"What happened to you?"

It was all I could say, I couldn't see any marks on him; there was no evidence of a car accident. I was confused. There was dried-up blood under his nose and in his ears. Then I saw the pool of blood under his head, which was still seeping from a wound. I later learnt that his skull was crushed but I couldn't see any evidence and neither did I want to.

It was not a good sight or image and not how I wanted to remember Boaz. As much as he had stripped me of my dignity and deceived me, I never wished him harm. I felt sorry for him and always will.

So many confusing thoughts were rushing through my head. I almost felt responsible for his death. I didn't kill him, but I believe I played a part in his death. If it wasn't for me Boaz would probably still be alive today. I could never hate Boaz; I forgave him a long time ago. Now it was time to say good- bye.

I reached for his hand and held it to my face; his hands were still warm. All the warm loving moments flashed back through my memory. I pictured us choosing our engagement ring; out running together. I could even hear his voice. But Boaz was gone forever. I put my arms around him. I wasn't afraid anymore. Joseph led me away but I felt weak and started to cry.

He took me into his office. He'd found a few things in Boaz's pockets and asked me if I wanted to look. Amongst his things was a handwritten letter addressed to me. I'd seen letters like this before. While we lived together in the bungalow off Nabe Road, we didn't speak to each other so he used to put notes under my bedroom door. They were often quite deep and full of contradictions. I used to call them love and hate notes. These letters would insist I'd got it all wrong. I wanted to believe him but reality told me otherwise. It was a far cry from the love notes Boaz used to slip into my bag. The sweet moments now, just memories.

I was also reminded of the papers Boaz had printed off the internet about anti-social personality disorder behaviour and sociopath disorder. I had seen these papers in the house and found their contents disturbing. I remember he was sitting at the computer desk, swinging his legs like a 5-year-old when I confronted him. He looked very vulnerable. We weren't even speaking to each other at the time. But I spoke to him from the heart and told him that if he was suffering from these symptoms, I would help and support him as a friend. His big, black eyes welled up as I reached out and offered my support.

Boaz had circled and highlighted some words and sentences:
Deception as indicated by repeatedly lying, use of aliases or using others for personal profit or pleasure.

This interest suggested that Boaz knew something wasn't right with him. Despite my own suffering, I couldn't hate him for his behaviour. I just knew I couldn't fix something Boaz wasn't willing to share. I had tried my best to reach out to him, like so many others. If I had stayed with him I would always be the victim and never the lover, wife or mother I wanted to be. Boaz got up from the chair and as he brushed past, he quietly said, "You can't help me, it's too late."

I had been at the mortuary about an hour and needed to go outside for some fresh air. Joseph led me through a maze of doors and then I was outside. I immediately puked up everywhere. He said I should call someone, maybe a friend. So I called Hannah.

"Sorry did I wake you? Boaz is dead." I heard a sharp intake of breath.
"What, how?"
"I don't really know. Some sort of car accident."
"What do you mean? Where are you?"
"At Mulago hospital."
"Have you seen him?"
"Yes."
"Oh my God."

Hannah is no fool and she was well aware of the trickery of some Ugandans. It has been known for some to fake their own death. But I don't think even Boaz could have played that one out. But wouldn't that have been the perfect con?

I needed to call Robert but his phone was switched off so I sent him a text. I needed to call Boaz's lawyer to let him know what had happened.

But it wasn't the lawyer who answered.

"This is Kira Road Police station."

"Oh, sorry I must have the wrong number."

"Is that Lisa?" The officer had recognised my English accent. I had been to the station so many times that most of the Officers knew me.

"Sorry, I thought I was calling Boaz's lawyer."

"You might be. I am so sorry about Boaz."

"You know already?"

"Yes, his car was in a road accident."

What did he mean by *his?* Joseph had said Boaz had died in a car accident but he didn't have a car. Our car was still in the CID HQ car park.

"But Boaz doesn't have a car."

"Well he was driving a Toyota Prado Land cruiser and it's been towed here. It's in the Police car park."

My stomach started to churn. "What, what colour was it?"

"Hang on a minute… white."

"Okay. Don't know whose car that is, maybe the other guy he was with."

"Oh, hold on. No, it's silver."

"What?"

"Can you read the registration number?"

He read it out. No, it can't be. That was my car: It was *the* car. What the hell is going on here? How had he got hold of the car? It was an exhibit in my court case and was supposed to be in the CID HQ car park.

"We are holding his lawyer at the station until we figure out what has happened."

"I want to speak to him."

"You cannot, he is drunk and asleep on the sofa. Why don't you come down here?"

"Okay, fine."

I called Hannah and told her about the car and said I was on my way to the police station. I would meet her afterwards. In the meantime, Bernard had called me. He was still at the hospital. He had waited for me. By now it was four in the morning. I was still in shock and got so lost trying to find my way back to Joseph that I ended up back in the mortuary. I came face to face with the man in the sheep jumper all over again. I clung onto the wall as I slid past him. I was so scared I started shouting for Joseph but he wasn't there. I shot through a door and spotted the corridor. I dashed through another door and up the spiral staircase that eventually took me back to reception. Bernard was there to greet me.

"Is it him Lisa?"
"Yes," it's him." I fell into his arms and then crashed onto the floor. I remember being on my knees, holding on to Bernard's legs. I was in total shock. As he helped me up, he stroked my hair and tried to comfort me.

"Please could you take me to the Kira Road Police Station? The car is there."
"Why is your car there?"
"I don't really know what is going on."

The journey was horrible and I felt too weak to hold on to the bike. Bernard had to stop on the way, for my own safety, when I broke down crying.

"Bernard, can you stay with me when we get to the Police station?"
"Yes, of course, I am not leaving you."

Bernard spotted the car first. It was parked at the front of the Police station on waste ground with other damaged cars.

"Lisa, your car." It was a shocking sight.

The roof was all caved in. Every panel was damaged and all the windows smashed. Apparently the car had rolled down the road a few times. Oh God. I assumed he had gone through the windscreen. But there was no evidence of that. At this point I had no idea exactly how Boaz had died but it wasn't in the car; that was for sure.

As I entered the Police station I saw his Idiot lawyer sitting on the sofa with his head flopped to one side. Boaz had got through a few lawyers during the case and had ended up with this drunk who worked for *Lukwago & Co.* So I went up to him and started poking. Nothing. Then I pulled at his suit. Still nothing. This guy was on another planet. I kicked his leg really hard but he never reacted. Two lady Police Officers were busy mopping the floor around me. They picked up his legs and mopped around him but he still didn't wake up. I could see there wasn't a mark on him. So how come Boaz is dead, with his skull crushed, and there's not a scratch on this guy? I kicked him again and got right up close to his face.

"Why is Boaz dead? Why is my car destroyed and why are you drunk? You're supposed to be looking after him, not getting him killed."

I remember grabbing him by his suit collar and calling him a bastard. "Boaz is dead?" he mumbled.

I was as angry as hell. I shouted more abuse but Bernard took me away and told me not to waste my time. The Police never interfered. They knew me and left me get on with it. The Police Officer I'd spoken to was not there but the Traffic Cop that had dealt with the accident was. I spoke to him in his office and he was very nice and very sympathetic. I asked him what had happened as nothing made sense.

"I'm waiting for the report from the other Officer as it doesn't look straight forward. The car appears to have come down the bank, fallen and rolled onto the road below."

"Where?" He told me the road. "Yeah, I know where that is. It's close to my house; near the underpass, not far from where my friend Hannah lives." The accident had been reported after midnight but he didn't have any more details.

I hesitated. "Was he murdered?"
"I don't think so," he replied. "He was found on the road, not in the car.

All I did was put him in the truck."
"A truck? In the back of a truck?" I was horrified.

With that his phone rang and he was called out to another accident. "I will call you later and we can discuss it further."

I was more and more confused. I hated the fact that Boaz had ended up in the back of a truck. Exactly the same as the boys we had seen on that rainy day in Mbarara, on the way back from our trip to see the Gorillas.

It was light now. Bernard took me straight home and he went to find Jackie to tell her what had happened. I knocked on Charlotte's bedroom window.

"What is wrong Muzungu?"
"Boaz is dead."
"What? What? What happened? Hold on. Let me get dressed and I will come to yours."

I was lying on my sofa crying when Charlotte arrived. She listened as I told her Boaz had died in a car accident. She was astonished. And shocked he'd called just minutes before he died.

"Oh My God Lisa, so many unanswered questions."

Charlotte called her boss to tell him she wouldn't be in that day. I was still shaking and couldn't stop smoking. I was lighting one cigarette with another cigarette. I kept asking myself why this was happening to me. And I couldn't stop crying.

And then Jackie came around and the local people I knew from Nabe Road. Even people I didn't know that well turned up to offer their condolences. That's the true meaning of kindness; the Ugandans are like this. Everyone was really supportive but I was still crying and crying. It was exactly two years to the day since Boaz had asked me to marry him - 6th August 2013. Calling me just before midnight, just to hear my voice, is something I will never forget as long as I live.

I was in a daze and I had this need to see where he had died. It was still very confusing about the car. No one could understand why or how he was driving our car. So we all agreed to meet at Jackie's and Bernard would take me to the shops to get some flowers. When Jackie asked why I needed flowers, I told her I wanted to lay some flowers at the crash site. I explained that maybe it's a British thing but when someone dies on a road, people lay flowers. It was where they took their last breath.

Boaz had died not far from the house. I could walk there in a few minutes. It sounded like he really must have been on his way over. Jackie and about twenty other people took the walk with me. By the time we got there another twenty people had joined us to see what was happening.

The accident had happened on Majwala Road. There is a Police post there and it leads to the Northern bypass. Boaz and I used to go running along that road. It was hard to make out how the car had overturned. There was a huge blood stain. It was clear from the amount of blood that Boaz had landed there, hit his head and never moved again. It was like someone had thrown some red paint and it had travelled over 15 meters toward the Underpass. The scene was quite shocking.

The traffic was building up and one of the boda-boda guys used long reeds of grass to mark the road so the cars could go round. I bent down and put my hand in the blood, hoping it wasn't real. But it was. The blood was sticky and I smeared it on my t-shirt. I was hysterical and it was all too much to take in. The guys helped me tie the flowers to the embankment. We all gathered round and Julius said a prayer. It was very moving and I was very grateful. The flowers had drawn a lot of attention and the media had arrived from the local TV station. I'd seen enough so asked Bernard to take me home.

Somehow local media had got into the compound and were asking for a few words. Reluctantly I agreed, "Okay, but no video." They asked for a photo of Boaz and were asking all sorts of questions when I noticed that one of the cameras had a light on and they were filming me. Julius then asked them to leave and got rid of them. They said they would run everything past me before they placed anything in the papers. But they never did. That night it was on TV. My friend Elizabeth called me but I couldn't speak. She texted me saying that she had seen it on the TV along with Boaz's picture. Then other Ugandans who knew me called saying the same thing. I never looked at any of the papers; it was too upsetting.

There was so much about Boaz's death that didn't make sense. The lawyer was obviously drunk but Boaz hadn't sounded drunk on the phone. And how had he got hold of the car? Robert had applied to the courts to have it removed, well away from that Susan. Neither Robert nor I was notified that Boaz had been handed the car. It was an exhibit in a court case. So did he steal the car from the CID HQ? The details of how exactly Boaz died was still a mystery. But not for much longer.

At 10.00 that night Jackie turned up with a young man who wanted to speak to me. This guy had been looking for 'the wife of Boaz.' At first Jackie had turned him away. She was very protective and thought it might be more media. But when he said he'd witnessed the accident, Jackie brought him round.

From the moment he started talking I knew he was telling the truth. This explained why there were no marks on Boaz's face. And why there was still so much blood at the scene.

He was a young guy and was on his way home from work when he saw the car hanging off the embankment. He was very nice and it was kind of him to come and see me. He felt I needed to know Boaz's last moments.

Boaz had been coming down this little back road which was a short cut for boda-boda bikes; it was like a grass embankment and leads to the highway. You can't drive a car down there because it's too narrow. But Boaz had tried to drive this great big 4 x 4 down it. The car had got stuck over this 9-foot drop. Half of the car was on the narrow path and half was hanging over with the front wheels spinning. Some boda-boda guys had stopped to help and were trying to push the car backwards onto the narrow pathway but they couldn't get a proper grip, so nothing was moving. The road isn't far from the Police post but none of the Officers came to help. They probably saw the lights and thought there goes another idiot.

The lawyer had somehow managed to crawl his way out of the car, and perched himself on the grass on the other side of the road. But Boaz had stayed in the car, still persevering. The young guy continued to tell me that Boaz got out of the car and had a look around to see how he could position the car. He had a joke with the boda-boda guys, got back in the car and then slammed it into revers. But the car hit the bank so hard that it shot forward. All the boda-boda guys ran as the car started to topple down the embankment. The nose of the car hit the road, rolled over and over and ended up on the other side of the road, half way in a ditch. Incredibly it landed upright.

Everyone was asking, where's the guy who was driving the car? No one could see him. But there he was, laid in the road. This young guy went over to check Boaz but he wasn't breathing. The lawyer came over and started shaking him. "Wake up, wake up." Only minutes before the lawyer had been shouting how he was a lawyer and this was his client. This young man ran to the Police station to tell them to come and hurry as there'd been an accident. The police came to check but Boaz was dead so they called the Traffic cops.

He continued. "I waited with him until the Traffic cops came but it was another hour before they turned up. While I was waiting one of the boda-boda guys shouted to the lawyer, if you're a lawyer, why are you both drunk? This is your fault."

I was still slightly confused. 'Okay, but how did Boaz end up in the road?"
"It looks like he tried to jump out of the car to escape but somehow he landed on his head and that's how I found him."

By the time the traffic cops came, the boda-boda guys had all disappeared.

Boaz had lay there for at least an hour and a half before a truck came to take him away. That's why there was so much blood. That stain remained on the road for over three months.

Hearing all this was really upsetting and I couldn't stop crying. It hurt like hell but at least I knew.
His uncle called me the next day to discuss the funeral.

"We need to bury him as soon as possible. The funeral will be in a couple of days in the village. If you are not going to the funeral you can pay your last respects at the mortuary, then you don't have to come all the way out to the village."

When someone dies in Uganda it's a quick burial. They don't have the refrigeration facilities like the UK. I wasn't sure how I'd get to the village for the funeral so reluctantly I went back to the mortuary.

Darius was sitting outside with one of the aunties. Hannah and Cecelia had warned me that I needed to be really careful now. This was a dangerous situation for me. I couldn't understand why but they said his family will look for someone to blame. And as an outsider and a foreigner, already taking Boaz to court, I was an easy target.

Darius just nodded in acknowledgement but the auntie was very pleasant and said if I needed someone to talk to she was there for me. She asked if I was going to the funeral.

"That's why I'm here. I've already been here once but I wanted to say goodbye as I don't know how I'm going to get to the funeral."
"Well, you can come with us if you want."
"That's very kind of you." But I hadn't yet made up my mind.
I thought it was unlikely that people would blame me for Boaz's death. After all, I wasn't there; surely they would know this.

The uncles were coming that afternoon to take Boaz's body and bring it back to the village. So if I chose not to go to the funeral, this was my last chance to say goodbye.

Boaz was now in a coffin with a glass top so you could just see his head. I wasn't scared like before but still I cried a tear that dropped onto the glass. He was dressed in a suit and his eyes were slightly open. He would have hated that suit; he had so many nice suits, why didn't they put him in one of them? I put my arms around the coffin and said goodbye. There were other coffins around but his was on the floor, not even on a pedestal or anything.

When I got home Boaz's sister, Rebecca called me.
"How are you?"
"I am alright." I wasn't quite sure what she expected me to say.
"Listen Lisa, I just wanted to ask what your plans are. Are you going to the funeral?"
"I think I might."

I hadn't been sure at first and it wasn't an easy decision. But I thought, no, I am going to stand tall and show my face. I haven't done anything wrong. And it's the devil I do and the devil I don't. Either way, I'll get criticized.

I could tell that wasn't the answer she was expecting to hear.

"Lisa, this is not really my business but you really need to keep off the alcohol."
"Excuse me."
"It is not a good image to turn up at the mortuary drunk to pay your last respects."
"What are you talking about?"

This is what they do. If you do anything they don't like they say you are drunk and tell everybody. The only thing I was guilty of was smoking a few too many cigarettes. This is what Boaz used to do, twist everything around to suit him. I asked her where she was getting this information from.

"The mortuary attendant told us."

Lies lies, even his sister lied. Who the hell was she, half my age, and trying to lecture me.

"Yeah, actually it is none of your business. I will see you at the funeral."

All she'd done was spur me on. I was sick of being intimidated by these people. I was going to his funeral.

Chapter Twelve

Devil I Do, Devil I Don't

His uncle called asking if I had any photos of Boaz. I had some in the house but had turned them all to the wall. I didn't want to get rid of them but I couldn't look at them. The uncle wanted a framed picture to put on top of the coffin.

"If you are going to come could you bring a photo?"

He was a bit frosty and I could hear in his voice that he had mixed feelings about me coming. I asked if he thought I would be safe at the funeral; after all what happened to Boaz wasn't my fault. He assured me I would be okay. I'd told Robert I was going but he'd also said I should be careful. I didn't know what he meant. When you are in the middle of a situation you don't really see how dangerous it is because it's your situation. But when you're on the outside, looking in, you can see things a hell of a lot clearer. How right they all were.

Jackie and Bernard and a few others left for the funeral at six in the morning. They got a taxi to town and then another taxi to the village. It was a long journey but they wanted to support me. Enoch had kindly arranged for two of his male friends to take me and Charlotte, as he was concerned for my safety. The day didn't get off to a good start. We'd been travelling for a good three hours when we got a flat tyre which meant we were extremely late. Jackie was already there and frantically texting me to say the funeral had started.

At least his uncle knew we were running late as I'd kept him posted by text. The funeral was being held at an uncle's house and Boaz was to be buried with other relatives next to the house, as they had their own burial site.

When we eventually got there I was greeted in the parking area by a relative that I had met before.

"Welcome home Lisa."

"Thank you."

But it didn't feel much like home to me.

I had never seen so many people in my life; masses and masses. It was like a crowd at a football match. The uncle was already standing up giving his speech so this young man guided us to our seats.

Chairs were dotted all around and Boaz's coffin was in the middle and draped with flowers. I had brought a single rose from Charlotte's rose bush and a few flowers from our own garden and wrapped them in a bit of silver foil. Boaz loved flowers and had planted these ones along with some herbs in our garden.

The young man took the framed picture and went round showing it to everybody then placed it on the coffin.

I remember it was so hot and the funeral seemed to go on for hours; along with the speeches. Some were in English and some in Ugandan. All the speakers were using microphones so you could hear every word. I was sitting behind some of the aunties, who were in the front row. Half way through the speeches one of them leant back and asked if Boaz had any children.

"Not that I knew of." It wouldn't have surprised me but no children ever turned up. It reminded me that anything is possible in Uganda – *TIA - This is Africa.*

Darius was now making a speech but I didn't understand a word he was saying. And then Isaac got up. I think he deliberately spoke in English so I'd understand every word.

"I last saw Boaz on the Sunday and he was in the car. I told him to put the car away for safety reasons."

What the hell? I nudged Charlotte. "Did you hear that? You're telling me he had the car all the time? All the time it was supposed to be under police custody, he's been driving around in it."

It sounded to me like someone, probably that Susan, had let him drive the car whenever he wanted. Isaac carried on.

"I was going to be a witness in his court case. Boaz was a good guy and none of this was his fault. Boaz never disrespected anyone."
Oh my God, is he for real? You stand up and say stuff like this at a funeral?

I was in total shock and disgusted. I could feel myself shrinking into my seat. Charlotte and I kept looking at each other. Did he really just say that? But it was about to get much, much worse.

Next up was Boaz's other brother Benjamin, the Immigration lawyer. He said all these nice things about Boaz. And then he looked directly at me.

"This is a message for Lisa. I notice you have only just bothered to get here. It is only because we are a Christian family that you are here in the first place. Otherwise you would not be welcome."

I'd say there were about four hundred people there and now four hundred pairs of eyes were all looking at me. I wanted to bury myself in that bloody hole they'd just dug. But I didn't cry. I was done with crying, I had no tears left. This meant nothing to me. I didn't care about this Benjamin and his spiteful words. I looked down. I thought okay, if that's how you want to play it.

I knew that Boaz's family had taken sides. Some blamed me for Boaz's death while others said it was a freak accident. But I never expected to be named and shamed in public.

Everyone stood as the coffin was picked up and lowered into the ground. I couldn't really see much of what was going on as there were so many people in the way. I wanted to hide but it's a bit difficult when you're the only Muzungu at a funeral. I didn't feel that emotional anymore as I think I'd got used to the situation after the shock of seeing him in the mortuary.

The two guys who'd accompanied me were getting uncomfortable and said we should leave. By now they'd started covering the coffin with dirt. I made my way over to the grave and said my last farewell to Boaz. Then I went to say goodbye to Anne, Boaz's sister and his uncle Mugisha. I'd always got on well with her and hoped that hadn't changed. Anne stayed in the village while her children were at school in Kampala; the school wasn't far from me. I used to visit them and take a few supplies. The school was a bit dingy but it was one of the better ones. It was a boarding school but very basic and the accommodation wasn't of a very high standard. I used to say let me know if the kids need anything. Once, Anne couldn't go to the parents' evening so the kids asked if I would like to come on her behalf. They were great kids. They were in the middle of their exams so Mugisha didn't want them to come to the funeral.

Anne was crying and I tried to console her. She said she was sorry for the cruel words and she didn't blame me for anything. Charlotte and Jackie both wanted to leave but then I spotted Benjamin. And he spotted me. I didn't have anything to hide and I wasn't afraid of his words; let him believe what he wants to. I was very nervous as I walked up to him and said, "Thank you for the kind words," and shook his hand and then walked away. I could feel the tension but believe it was more a family issue rather than a 'me' issue.

Charlotte couldn't understand why I'd been so nice. "Why did you shake his hand after he said those awful things about you?"
"It makes me the better person."
"Good job you didn't arrive earlier," said Jackie.
"What do you mean?"
"These people were standing up and slandering you and calling you a white witch. One of the uncles even said this Muzungu is bad news and only after Boaz's money."
"Really?" But then *TIA - This is Africa* and I was past caring.

My friends had made a big effort to come with me and I wanted to say thank you. I suggested we stop and eat; my treat. I told them to order whatever they wanted. It was the first time I'd eaten a proper meal for months and months. I couldn't remember if I'd eaten from one day to another. I'd lost weight but all of a sudden I found my appetite. I wanted to eat everything. I felt completely different, like a great big weight had been lifted off my shoulders. I was convinced everything was going to be alright. The court would rule in my favour and I would get my money back. And I'd sell the car and the land. I was still sad but everything was going to be alright now.

After the funeral I had to go back to court. Boaz was buried on the Friday and we had been due in court that day. But now things had changed so Robert and I made an appointment to see the Judge. He was unaware that Boaz had died and was shocked.

Boaz's lawyer didn't turn up to address the Judge. He had spent a few days in jail and made a statement. He didn't go to the funeral either. Amazingly he didn't get any blame for Boaz's death.

My evidence had been due to finish on the Friday and the Judge would have delivered his judgement soon after. Who would have thought the court case would end up this way? Despite everything I still wanted what was mine.

The Judge was now flicking through his legal books. "I have never had anyone die half way through a court case. This will be a first." There was no precedent to follow so he wasn't sure what to do. He decided to put the case on hold and it would be reopened when Boaz's family came forward to make a claim. They would need to present themselves to the court and state whether they wanted to continue with the case.

I'd had to make a statement to the Police about Boaz's phone call before he died. I'd found out that Boaz had died just twenty-five minutes after I spoke to him. The police were very kind but explained they needed to clear me of any involvement in his death. While the Police were out of the room I noticed the file about Boaz's death, just lying there. Well, of course, I had to have a look. I flicked through and found the lawyer's statement and started reading it. He claimed he'd had nothing to do with picking up the car from CID Headquarters. All he knew was that Boaz had called him. "Let's go out." Boaz picked him up from his office and they'd gone for a couple of drinks. Yeah, and the rest.

I saw Boaz's lawyer a couple of months later. He tried to talk to me, as if nothing had happened. He welcomed me and went to shake my hand but I declined. You must be kidding me. I was done with him and every other bent person in this country. I know he wasn't driving but did he really advise Boaz, his client, in the best possible way?

The Judge had suggested I complain about this lawyer's misconduct. "We can't have lawyers running round drunk with their clients." Robert told me to forget about it but I felt I had to make a complaint of some sort. Surprise, surprise there was nothing anyone could do. Yes, he was drunk but he was a passenger; he hadn't been driving. It didn't matter if he was drunk or not which, sadly, was true.

Normally I only spoke to the Judge through my lawyer but now he addressed me directly, as if Robert wasn't there.

"I don't mean to be insensitive Miss Morgan but I think you have had a lucky escape. I knew exactly where this case was going. But now he is dead, you need to move on with your life and get out of this country. This is an unbelievable story and would make an excellent book. You cannot imagine how many people have been asking me about your case."

I couldn't believe what I was hearing but I'd always known that Justice Benjamin Kabiito was a good Judge. He had been sensitive towards me from the beginning; protecting my privacy from the press. As a Muzungu he knew I was vulnerable and how much in love I was with this man. He had been a brilliant Judge. Keen to get the case wrapped up, he'd even come in on his day off and cancelled his holiday. "Somehow you will find a way." I will always be grateful to him.

Life was a blur but I needed to focus. I still felt sad but I had the car and the land; I could sell them and then decide what to do next. I needed a copy of Boaz's death certificate to reclaim the car but couldn't get one. I wasn't a relative and despite everyone calling me his wife, we weren't actually married. Someone suggested I call some General who was a relative of Boaz; he'd signed the death certificate. Forget it; his family weren't going to help me and neither did I want to be frustrated by anyone. And I knew the family were after the car. Although it was damaged, it was still worth something. It had all four wheels and the engine was still okay. The windows and panels might be smashed but it was all repairable. Ugandans are resourceful people and will find a way.

I told Robert to write a letter to the Judge, asking him to sign the car over to me. But he said he couldn't, we had to wait to see what Boaz's family were going to do. But as I was a registered Company Director, and the car was in the company name, I could get the car back. The car had been towed away to a different Police pound now, where wrecked cars go for inspection after an accident. Then they are either reclaimed or crushed. I'd contacted the Insurance Company to let them know the car had been in an accident and Boaz had died. And put in a claim. There were a few forms to fill in which they would email to me. Then they called back. There was still an outstanding amount to pay.

I couldn't believe it. All that money he had stolen yet he hadn't even paid all the car insurance.

I went to the Police pound with an Insurance broker who took some photos of the car. He explained I had to pay the outstanding amount before the company would pay out. It was 1.8 million Ugandan Shillings, approximately £363. Where was I going to find that kind of money? I needed time. Before all this I could see some light at the end of the tunnel. But now it felt as if the walls were shrinking in on me again.

Everything was taking so long. It was October when the Judge finally agreed to release the car. But it still wasn't mine.

The said Director, Morgan Lisa, to maintain and preserve the said vehicle until the resolution of the High Court Civil Suit No 21 of 2013 or until the court orders otherwise.

I would still have to come to some kind of settlement with the family. The uncle had told me the family had been to see the car and they wanted it. They'd even tried to take it away but the police had refused to release it. I'd had to pay a towing company to bring the car to the house but that wasn't easy either. They wanted their money upfront. They'd picked cars up before and never got their money.

"Now you listen to me. I have been through shit. I am not going to let you down. I need you to bring the car. And you are going to pick it up and drop it at my house. And I am going to be there and I will pay you. Do you understand?

The guys could see I wasn't to be messed with. And after all, I was a Muzungu I could be trusted. But nothing in Uganda is straightforward and I was so drained by it all. When we went to pick up the car, someone had been busy. They had ripped out the Air Conditioning unit, the electric window switches and the CD player. I wasn't sure how much more I could take. I spoke to the Officer in charge. "Are you quite sure it wasn't missing when you brought it in here? You can make a claim if you think anything has been stolen." Oh my God. This was a Police compound; if your property wasn't safe there, where was it safe?

The car was now in the driveway, parked near the wall. It didn't look too bad. The roof was damaged but the roof rack had taken most of the impact. Yes, the windows and panels were smashed but it was all fixable. You can have a connection with a vehicle and I did have a connection with this car. I hated it. All the fights, the arguments we'd had over that car; the car that killed Boaz.

Somehow I scraped together the money. It took me about three weeks and I sold my sofa to pay for the outstanding insurance premium. A young girl from the Insurance Company was dealing with my claim. She'd come round to the house to take my payment and gave me a receipt.

A month later she was back. This time she brought someone with her; a bad sign.

"I have some good news and some bad news."

I didn't like those two words in the same sentence.

"I have got some money for you but only half of what your claim was."
"Why?"
"The insurance cover expired by the time you paid the premium. The insurance ran out during that time making it null and void."
"You've got to be kidding me? So you are telling me that I have given you over a million for nothing? You took the money off me knowing this. What is this, some kind of joke or a trick?" The frustration was going to kill me.

Because of the tragic circumstances they were prepared to give me something, but it was only half of what I was expecting. It was so unprofessional, it felt like a scam. The insurance had run out yet they still took my money. And I had a receipt to prove it. I went nuts and refused to accept it. They were at fault; they should have noticed. I went to see Trading Standards and they set up mediation sessions between my broker, the insurance company and me. I took my friend Robert with me as support. He had been really good to me and I trusted him. Everyone was arguing and blaming each other. I was getting nowhere.

I was advised to take the Insurance Company to court for breach of contract. What was the point of mediation if they couldn't enforce anything? But all this would take at least a year and I didn't have a year. Everything in Uganda was so slow.

Then I fell out with the Insurance broker. He was also the owner of the first apartment Boaz and I lived in. It is clear that when money is involved you see a different side to people. I think the broker expected me to lie down and take it. He turned his back on me and sent me a terrible email.

"If you want professional behaviour than you should act professionally."
Who the hell was he? You don't send clients emails like this but *TIA - This is Africa*.

The frustration was endless even with Boaz gone. Everyone had messed me about. I didn't have time for any more crap.

So I spoke to someone at the actual Insurance Company. He was very nice and a lot calmer. He thought that after all I had been through; I should consider taking the offer. He could write me a cheque there and then. The next morning, I decided to just take the money. Every little helps. If I hadn't had my twenty shares in the company, I would have been entitled to nothing I took the cheque and paid it into my account. At last I had some money.

That night I heard something. I wasn't able to see directly out the window so I opened the door and walked towards the car. I could see a light moving inside; someone was in the car. Oh, no. Somebody had jumped over the wall and got into the car and now they were taking stuff. I was too terrified to confront them. They could have been armed with a Machete. So I slipped quietly back into the house. In the morning I could see they'd taken the wing mirrors. These were expensive and much sought after. At this rate there would be nothing left of the car. Even the Judge had said I needed to get the car out of the Police compound as soon as possible, otherwise there wouldn't be much left. He knew his own people well. Funnily enough when the car was at the CID HQ compound, before the crash, it was next to *Bad Black's*. My car had remained intact while *Bad Black's* was smashed to pieces.

This car is a survivor. First it gets thrown down the road, tipped upside down and ends up in a ditch. Then the police steal stuff from it which, of course, I can't prove. Then somebody jumps over the wall and steals even more. At this rate I'd be lucky to get one Ugandan shilling for it. So the next day I went to the hardware shop and bought some big tarpaulin sheets and covered it up. I also moved it closer to the house; got some barbed wire and reinforced the top of the wall.

141

Peter was our cleaner and odd job man. He cleaned the houses in the compound and looked after the garden and cut the grass. We asked him if he would like to work as security. But he would have to sleep in the car as we didn't have a proper security out-building. I didn't want anything else stolen. Peter would arrive around 10 o'clock every night. He was married with a young family and I think he had another job during the day. He would sleep until 7am and leave when Charlotte left for work.

I'd stopped paying rent for now and told Cecelia that I needed time to get everything sorted. It was only $250 US dollars a month but I was struggling. The house had belonged to her husband's first wife who'd died. Cecelia was using the money to look after the deceased lady's children. It's quite common in Uganda for a family to look after the children, if a parent has passed away and I thought it was nice. Isaac, the Police lawyer, was looking after his brother's kids. There were ten kids in total.

The man from the water board had come round to read the meter and the reading was really high. Normally the bill was around 20 or 30 US dollars a month. But all of a sudden it jumped to 1.8 million. What? That was enough water to fill an Olympic sized swimming pool. Where the hell was all this water? The water board thought there might be a leak or we were selling it. That's the sort of thing people did. We wouldn't pay the bill until it was fixed and now the water had been cut off. We decided to sort it out ourselves and paid someone to fix it.

The bungalow was brand new but wasn't very well finished. Doors and knobs were still hanging off. One day I was having a shower when I noticed the water wasn't getting very hot and there was a burning smell. Then the boiler blew up. It turned out the heating system wasn't getting any water. Charlotte paid for it to be fixed. But whatever they did, they managed to cut off the water that supplied my water heater. Oh my God what next?

I now had to boil water on the gas stove to wash my hair and shower. I'd often seen rows of single mothers outside their small units. All the kids were running around naked while the ladies were doing the washing with big buckets of water. Laughing and joking and pouring water over their heads. Now this was me but I wasn't laughing.

We'd send Peter to fill up containers with water. He was only a little guy but was very tough and carried the container on his head. The Ugandans could carry pianos on their heads and that's just the women.

I called Boaz's sister Anne to arrange a meeting about my court case and to see if they were going to help. She said she couldn't afford the bus ticket so I sent her the money. I didn't have much but friends from the UK and America had sent me money so I had some spare cash. If it would get my situation sorted, then it was money well spent. I needed a member of the family to come forward. Anne was coming with the uncle and Boaz's brothers.

I spent the morning cooking lunch for them but they didn't turn up. Anne called much later and made some excuse we so we re-arranged for two weeks later. I had already sent the money. History was repeating itself. Two weeks felt like a lifetime. This time I made burgers with salad for lunch. The family turned up and apologised, someone had been sick but I didn't care. And now one of the brothers had backed out. He was on Benjamin's side and was clearly interested in what he could get out of it, not what he could do to help me.

Anne, poor Anne, was being criticized for even speaking to me. She didn't think the car looked too bad and had an idea to sell it. Even she was more interested in the money than helping me. I had to stick to my guns. I wasn't going to give in and share with them. I needed to pay what I owed in rent and to buy a ticket to the UK. I had to get the hell out of here.

Afterwards we sat down and looked over the papers I had drawn up. I said all I needed was a signature to say you are not interested or will not be making a claim regarding the car and the land. One of the brothers wanted to know what was in it for them. "Maybe we need to think about it?" They also wanted to speak to the village elders. So they left without signing. I felt like saying why didn't you say all this before? You've wasted my time and eaten my food.

Despite being a bit off with me before, the uncle had stayed in touch. He suggested I find another way. "I do not want anything from you Lisa. I just want you to be happy." Anne had tried to help me but she was weak and favoured her relatives. And she was surrounded by people who hated me and had no intention of signing the papers. Seeing the elders was just a delaying tactic. I was stuck.

Chapter Thirteen

Mother Nature Guide Me

Charlotte would come and see me virtually every night after she got home from work.

'" Muzungu are you there?"

"Yes I'm here."

I guess after my suicide attempt, and everything that had happened, she knew how hard it was for me. And remaining trapped in this country didn't help. I could 'cry me a river' but it wouldn't do any good. Most times I'd be hiding under my covers when she came round. I would lie there for hours and hours thinking of ways to get out of this situation. I had so many issues to sort out and the pressure was piling up.

I was always pleased to hear Charlotte's voice but I had nothing to say and felt so depressed. It was comforting to know I had somebody next door who cared for me. Charlotte was so reliable and supportive with a wise head on such young shoulders. She always said she did nothing but she did so much more than that. Sometimes it's enough just to have someone there.

She recently wrote me a letter.

Lisa, always remember that after the loss of Boaz you managed to keep going when you were going through the toughest of times. You were an innocent foreigner with such a big heart and someone just didn't appreciate that.

And you always looked out for me, ensured safety at my house when I was away. I'll forever be grateful. It was terrible for Boaz to die when you guys were still having some issues but I'm sure if he were still alive, he would have realized his mistake and discovered what a good soul you were.

Charlotte also knew about heartache. She'd told me a story once about when she was in love with this guy and was convinced that one day she would marry him. She didn't see him a lot but once she needed to see him urgently so went to his house. He was a bit off with her. She found out later that he had a wife and children in the village. "Lisa, I wanted to die on the spot."

Every day was a struggle. I would walk from one room, then into another and just stand still in a daze. I would break down all the time. I'd be making tea, cleaning my teeth or just in the middle of a conversation when a wave of emotion would engulf me. I kept having flashbacks of Boaz in the mortuary and could still feel the warmth of his hand. But feeling sorry for myself wasn't going to help my situation. Without Boaz's family coming forward and taking over the court case I was well and truly stuck in Uganda. The Judge wasn't going to just award me everything; it wasn't as easy as that.

Christmas had come and gone and every day was torture. Even Robert was at a loss about what to do. He told me to keep on trying with Boaz's family as without their consent it was virtually impossible to reach closure on my case. But the family weren't interested in taking on his case as they knew they would lose. His sister and the other brothers wanted too much; a share of the damaged car and the land. Why the hell should I give them anything? And anyway it wouldn't leave me with enough to fix my passport, visa or get a ticket out of Uganda.

The depression was like no other I had ever experienced. I could literally feel my brain being squeezed. I didn't speak to anyone for weeks and I even started to ignore the phone. I'd made a decision; I would cut myself off from everyone, even my dear friend Enoch. We used to speak every night on the phone: he would call me or I would call him. He was the only person I knew that was able to turn my sad tears into tears of laughter. But not anymore. I cut myself off from Hannah too which was really hard. I loved Hannah, she was strong, honest, and supportive and the best kind of friend anyone could wish for. But I didn't want to burden them anymore with my tears and to be honest, I was sick of hearing my own sob story.

I knew I needed to take back control of my life but I didn't know how. I'd given up smoking. I was sick of my hair stinking; the smell was so horrible. I'd been in the bathroom one day and looked at myself in the mirror with a cigarette in my hand. And I thought you know what, you look ugly with a cigarette. I asked myself why do you need to smoke? So I made up my mind, no more cigarettes.

I was so numb; I'd lost all track of time and didn't know what day it was from the next. I sometimes didn't sleep and would be wide awake before Charlotte had even left for work. I would make a cup of tea and sit outside and watch her leave. I was still sat in that same position when she came back from work. This went on for weeks; I was in a daze. One day a plastic bag had blown into the garden. I went to pick it up but the wind blew it away from me. I spent the rest of the morning watching it whooshing up and down the garden, being swept up by the wind and forming its very own mini tornado dance.

The only people I saw were Peter and Charlotte. I didn't leave the compound for months. When I did, it was only to pick up money friends had sent via the *Western Union*.

One day I was in the kitchen preparing some food. I was starting to eat more; I guess stopping smoking had given me an appetite. I was checking I hadn't left any crumbs that would attract cockroaches, before making my way into the living room. And then I saw something move.

The back door was not like the doors in the UK; it was a sheet of reinforced metal with a bolt across it. Most of the doors were like this to keep out thieves. The door was shut but not bolted and was an army green colour; most windows and doors in Uganda are painted that colour. As I walked towards the door I saw what looked like a sock wrapped around the handle. I looked closer and realised it was a snake. It was the same colour as the door and now it wasn't moving. I tried to stay calm but no way could I deal with this on my own so I called Julius.

"I have a snake in my kitchen."

"What colour is it?"
"What? Green, it's green."
"Is it on the loose?"
"No, it's wrapped around the handle of the back door."
"I am on my way, don't touch it."
 "Ha, no chance of that."

I think as I pulled the door shut it was on its way in. So now it was half in, half out. I think I must have half killed it. It made me feel squeamish. I don't know if it was poisonous but I wasn't taking any chances. I shut the kitchen door, in case the snake wriggled free, and stood standing on a chair in the living room and waited.

Julius was here in minutes and brought Ahmed with him. Ahmed was another boda-boda guy and lived nearby. He had taken me all over the place in Kampala. Once we both fell off his bike while crossing a muddy dirt track. I remember the bike got stuck in the mud and came to a standstill. We both fell off in slow motion and landed in the dirt. I laughed so hard and so did Ahmed.

I used to use about four or five boda-bodas. Another one was called Adolf. I'd asked him if that was his real name and he said it was. He was under 'H' for Hitler in my phone contacts and I used to make him laugh with a Nazi Salute whenever I saw him.

"Okay, where is it?"
"In the kitchen, still wrapped around the door handle. It's a very long snake."

They checked I was okay and then headed for the kitchen. I could hear all this commotion. "You get it, no you get it." They tried to bash it with my broom but broke the handle; blimey, don't destroy my kitchen.

Fifteen minutes later they both came out. "Okay, all done."

'Oh, really? Where is it?"

"We chopped its head off and threw it onto the roof of those smelly chickens," replied Julius. "Now make us a cup of tea."

Finding things to pass the time, while Robert figured out a way forward, was painful. I'd often sit in front of the mirror telling myself that everything would be okay. I found these pretty butterfly grips in the bottom of my make-up bag. I'd bought them while out shopping with Rita in Lebanon. They reminded me of the happy person I was back then and they made me smile. For a brief moment I felt beautiful instead of this ugly, foolish person; then I ripped out the hair grips and threw them across the room. Everything was taking so long that it was driving me nuts. I spent a lot of time on the patio; night after night. Sometimes I'd call Robert, my lawyer, but I could hear in his voice that he was at a loss.

During the day all I could hear was the kettle being switched on, the washing machine or the opening of the fridge door. In my head there was nothing, only silence. It was like I was dead inside. And at night all I heard was the crickets. All those sounds seemed really loud to me and I barely spoke as there was no one to speak to. Nearly all my speaking was inside my head. I spent all of my time at home and rarely ventured out to Jackie's shop anymore.

The compound was enclosed. I was surrounded by large houses from the back and side and a 7ft wall separating the view but not the smell from those smelly chickens. Leading from my front door was a covered patio area with my table and chairs. Even when it rained I could sit outside, sheltered from the rain. There was a small garden with a lawn and a beautiful rose bush and a small avocado tree. Boaz had laid stepping stones which led to Charlotte's front garden and the main gate. I loved living there; it was private, very beautiful and large enough for two bungalows. This was my world; behind a seven-foot wall.

The big house had a maid and one day she was singing away as she hung out the washing. I couldn't understand what she was saying but it sounded really sweet. It made me realise how lonely and isolated I had become; I slowly walked over to the wall and listened to her happiness. I remember having my back to the wall, sliding down it and sitting there crying. Why couldn't that be me singing on the other side of that wall? I was scared to leave the compound. I had made myself a prisoner of my own security.

I was in a bad way physically too. My hands and feet had become swollen. The stress of everything was catching up with me. Of course, I had no TV to keep me company, only my laptop and my Sony compact stereo. I'd had it for years but it still sounded brilliant. I couldn't find much on the radio so I used to play my CDs. A lot of the time the house was silent but when I played my CDs it was always at full blast. *Pink Floyd, Blondie, Billy Idol* and *Metallica*. I emptied a whole box onto my living room floor and played one CD after another. I didn't listen to any sad stuff. It only made me cry. I'd dance around the house, jump on the chair and then run into the bedroom and jump on the bed. Peter would see me sometimes through the netted curtains, when he was gardening but I didn't care. I'd laugh out loud but I was laughing alone.

I wondered if this is how madness started. Was this the beginning of a slippery slope for me? Especially, as the laughter always ended in tears. I'd lie on my bed and scream, "I hate my life, I hate my life."

But it was music and nature that helped me hang on. When I first arrived in Uganda I'd been amazed by the different types of species. I love nature and nature was my salvation. I spent days watching the wildlife in the garden, so different from back in the UK. Butterflies are huge in Uganda and their brightly coloured wings made them look more like flowers floating in the air. Whenever I'd see one in the garden I'd point and say, "Peter look, look." He would laugh his head off. I was obsessed with Butterflies. Once, Boaz chased around the garden with a camera in his hand, to take a photo of a Butterfly just for me. I still have that picture. So often Boaz would give me whatever I wanted; that was the Boaz I knew.

Peter was lovely and you could trust him. His English wasn't too good but we somehow communicated. On a Saturday Peter would be around all day, cleaning our houses, washing Charlotte's clothes and cutting the grass. He was a hard worker so for lunch I would make him a fried egg sandwich and hot tea and put it outside. He was so pleased. "Thank you Madam," he would say.

Peter would leave and then come back at night time to do the security for us. I would give him hot water in a flask so he could make some tea during the night. I'd say good night and see if he needed anything else before I went to bed. Often I would be distracted by the brightness of the stars. "Wow, look at that Peter, a shooting star." The stars were amazing in Uganda and the moon was so big it felt like you could reach out and touch it. No street light pollution or cloud to get in the way.

Nature's visitors to my garden were a Godsend. It was a rare opportunity for me to see such natural beauty close up. A blue Dragonfly perched itself regularly on my wall. I used to go right up to it but it never moved. I really wanted to touch it but it looked so delicate. Then it would buzz off. The next day it was back again, stuck on the same wall and I would say hello. Sometimes I only spoke to the Dragonfly.

Then there were the lizards. There was an orange and blue tailed lizard that lived somewhere in the back of my garden. And some black tailed lizards that used to sit inside the vented bricks in my bathroom. They were covered with wire mesh and were supposed to stop bugs and lizards getting in. But these lizards used to hide inside and sometimes their tails would poke out. It used to freak me out. I also avoided going in there because it had once been Boaz's bathroom. And I could still feel his presence.

This blue lizard was about a foot long; his sheer size and bright colour used to stop me in my tracks. Sometimes he would be sitting on the wall outside my back door, waiting for his next meal. I found him quite intimidating and we used to stare at each other. Then he'd scamper off. But after months of seeing him we got used to each other and he would stay around, basking in the sun looking smug.

I would get the odd cockroach in the house and I hated them. They were huge. Charlotte had them too and she used kick them with her feet which

I hated. I'd scream, "Please don't do that." I didn't even like taking a pee in the bathroom if there was one in there. They made me squeamish.

One day I spotted a cockroach in the kitchen. Much as I disliked them, I didn't want to kill it. The back door was open so I got hold of my broom and held it like an ice hockey stick. I hit the cockroach and it went flying out the door, straight into the jaws of my local neighbourhood lizard. Goal! I was laughing. I swear to God this is how I used to amuse myself.

I was also rather taken by this huge bird called the Marabou stork. I'm not talking about the nice white storks that deliver new-born babies! This stork stands about 4-foot-tall, with a head like a bald eagle, a straggly turkey neck and wings that expanded to 8 feet wide. Not exactly nature's best looking birds. In fact, they are known as The Undertaker bird, because from the back they look like a huge cloak. I'd spend hours sitting in the garden watching these huge birds soaring thousands of feet high in the sky. I don't think I've ever seen anything so prehistoric. I swear it was just like a scene out of *Jurassic Park*.

Even in downtown Kampala you could see them exploiting these urban areas and scavenging amongst the garbage dumps. I was a bit fearful of them, especially when I was sitting in my regular spot at the *Khyber Pass, Speke Hotel*. I would see them perching high in the trees; the perfect take-off point to swoop down and snatch a morsel from my plate. I just hoped we didn't share the same taste in food or I would be out of luck.

One morning I was sat outside with my regular cuppa when I noticed these damn ants; bloody ants everywhere. So I got some ant killer and started exterminating them. But they kept coming back morning after morning, they were relentless. I spotted yet another ant trail so got down on the ground to see where they were going. I could see them marching together, carrying a dead locust. I got some water and poured it over their pathway to see what they would do. One stopped and they all stopped. It was as if they were talking to each other. "Right men, we have a problem here." They were like little soldiers. I watched, fascinated.

I so admired these ants. They had kept coming back even though I was trying to kill them. They worked together as a team. If there was an obstacle they'd find a way round it. I was going to leave them alone. These ants had inspired me to find the strength to move forward. To get over all those hurdles. If they can do it, I can do it. So I wrote a list of the things I had to do.

First on the list was a new passport. There was no room left for any more stamps in my old one. And even if there was, I didn't have a valid visa. A while back I had given my passport to Boaz's brother Benjamin to sort out but he never did. And after his speech at the funeral he wasn't going to help me now. Luckily Sean, a lifelong friend of mine, had kindly agreed to pay for a new passport. It cost £250 so wasn't cheap. The closest country to Uganda that would issue a new passport was South Africa. Sean contacted the British Embassy in Uganda and paid by credit card.

I needed a new photo so I went to the Metroplex Centre near to my house. When I got to the photo shop I saw the boy that worked in there. "Madam, madam, I am so sorry about your husband." He had taken pictures of me and Boaz in the past. I asked him to take some passport photos for me and he did. Then I sat with him as he uploaded the photos onto his computer. As he flicked through the photos to find mine, I saw a picture of me.

"Hold on, that's me. How did you get that picture of me?"
"From your husband. He came in with a thumb drive and asked me to print it."

This picture was from my Facebook page. No one else had that picture. He must have copied it. Why would he do that? It was a wallet sized picture and the boy said he printed it for him after February 2013. I couldn't understand why he would be bothered to have a picture of me, unless he wanted to use it for dart practice. Things were bad between us then, however I had a picture of him in my purse. I hadn't thought about throwing it away; photos are a funny thing to deal with and right now I had more important things to deal with. I kept learning new things about Boaz, even though he was dead. And I still didn't really understand him.

It took about three weeks to finally get my shiny new passport and it was a great feeling when the Embassy called to say come and collect it. You can't imagine how brilliant that was. It was a small step but it was a step in the right direction. The passport was so precious to me. The next hurdle was to sort out my visa and that would cost more money. The problems I faced were never-ending.

To stay in Uganda, you need a valid visa. If Boaz and I had got married this wouldn't have been a problem. I'd managed to get it renewed three times before to keep myself legal. Robert had told me I was okay as I had a court case; it was in my interest to stay in the country until it was sorted. My visa had run out a long time ago and there was no way I was paying a $50 US dollars fine for every month I'd been without a visa. This would use up all my car insurance money.

I told Hannah I would have to spend all my money to fix my visa.

"I know a guy that could help. I will give you his number and he can sort it out." I was surprised. But then she had been in Uganda for a long time. "Well, *TIA - This Is Africa,*" and we both laughed.

So I met this guy in a coffee bar. I told him my story and showed him my passport. He took one look and knew exactly what needed to be done. He said he could fix it. I didn't ask how; it was better not to know the details. I was anxious and prayed I would see him again. Now all I could do was wait.

He was as good as his word and I got my passport back after three weeks. I could see it had been on its own little vacation without me. All the dates were sorted and I was legal again. I had months before I needed to renew it again. Now there was nothing to stop me leaving. I just needed to sort out some money for a ticket and think about sorting out my life when I get back to the UK.

The business with the car was still a mess. To me the Police were liable for releasing the car back to Boaz. It was an exhibit in my court case but now it was all smashed up. No one was helping me; no one wanted to take responsibility. I knew I needed to do something; I had to get out of this situation. But what could I do? I was trapped in a waiting game. Julius came to my rescue. We'd become good friends. We had the same sense of humour and he seemed to understand me. We'd smoke a 'funny' cigarette together. At least it stopped me from crying.

"Lisa, I am younger than you and do not really want to advise you. I know you do not trust us Africans that much but we are not all like that. You are a law-abiding citizen and I get that but look what has happened to you."
"What do you mean?"

"You are a good person, a lovely person and it hurts me to see you go through all this. You thought you could trust the Police but they have messed it all up and let you down. The man who said he loved you took all your money and left you to starve. No one here will care if you are a law-abiding citizen or not. You need to do whatever it takes to get out of this situation. Go back to your country and start again."

I was hearing a few home truths. Julius had planted a seed. He was right. There is a predator at the top of every food chain and I felt I'd been eaten alive.

That night I started to write a plan of action. If no one is going to help me then I will help myself. First the car and then I would tackle the land. So I asked Julius to find a buyer for the car. I gave him some taxi money and that very same day he brought someone round. We struck a deal and the very next day he came with a truck and took it away. I was glad to see the back of it. With more money in my bank account I felt I had a bit of power. Perhaps this is how Boaz had felt.

Charlotte and I still needed Peter to take care of security. I didn't feel a hundred per cent safe in the house and I liked having him around. Now the car was gone so he had nowhere to sleep. I couldn't afford to build a brick shelter for him so bought him a tent. I'd never seen anyone so happy when I gave it to him. He put the tent up in the corner of the garden; he was so happy. Charlotte said I spoilt him but I was worried about Peter sleeping in a tent. And some nights it rained so hard that I thought Peter and his tent would be washed away down Nabe Road.

I'd got rid of the car. Now it was time to get rid of the land. If his family want to stop me, let them show their faces in court. I was ready.

Chapter Fourteen

On the Road to Survival

Like everything else the land was in Boaz's name. And like the car, it wasn't going to be easy to get rid of. I'd got to know this guy called Milton who lived near my plot of land. He was an older gentleman and the kind who knows everybody and knows everything that's going on in the village. I really liked him and he always had a smile. He'd helped me while I was briefly building my house on the land.

I called him and explained I needed to fix a problem. I took a boda-boda to the city and we sat down and discussed it. He said if I was serious he would meet with the councilor's and organize a meeting. First thing he suggested was putting a Security Guard on the land. It wouldn't be difficult for Boaz's family to snatch the land away, as it was still in his name; even though I had a court case against him, claiming it back. But *TIA – This is Africa*. They could always find a way to make it difficult for me. His brother had already tried to claim my car from the Police, after the crash; as if he had the right. None of them could be trusted. Look what happened to my car when it was in Police custody? I didn't care if my land was in his name; it was just another one of his scams and I was determined to get it back. So I put a Security Guard in place but none of his family ever came. I later found out that Boaz had actually bought land in the village, a few boda-boda bikes and lent money - 'my money' - to a lawyer who had gone to work in Dar es Salaam, so wasn't returning anytime soon. Let them fight over that; as long as they kept their nose out of my business.

I didn't tell Robert, my lawyer, what I was doing. He'd been good enough to get me this far but I needed to make the rest of my journey alone. The Police had messed up my case and by releasing my car from Police custody; they had contributed to Boaz's death. Now they just hid themselves away and left me to pick up the pieces. However, the Police who did help me were brilliant and did their best. It's just a shame there weren't more like them.

Milton spoke to the local Council and explained the situation. They were well aware of who I was as one of the councilor's used to come down and say hello to me when I was building the house. They knew it was my money that had paid for the land. Also the original copies of the agreement had my signature so that helped. There were about six councilors' and they knew every single house and every single person in that village. Nothing escaped them. If you wanted to buy or sell a house, you had to go and see them. I had total faith in Milton. He would help fix it for me.

Of course, *TIA – This is Africa* so I knew it would cost me. Milton told me to put some money aside. He knew I was struggling and the land was quite a distance from my house so he came with a friend and collected me which I thought was really nice of him. There was only the land to discuss. The house walls had collapsed as it never got its roof. Boaz had stopped the build and the weather had pretty much destroyed it.

The councilor's offices were off the main road, down a dusty old track. I was sat at the back while Milton spoke to the councilor's and organized everything. Obviously they wanted to be sure that Boaz was dead, even though a few of them had seen it on TV, so I showed them a copy of the traffic accident report. They were very nice to me and sympathetic but then, they too had something to gain. There were lots of discussions and Milton was translating for me. Although they could speak English, their accent was very strong. I signed some papers, slid over an envelope and it was done.

They'd already found a buyer for the land but there was a catch. I had to sell it for a certain price to a certain woman. I had already lost so much but now I was ready to leave the country at any price. This small piece of land, that cost more than 35 million Ugandan shillings, around £7,000, was sold for a quarter of its original value; as was the car. I was so drained by it all. But at least it was gone. One less thing to worry about.

Milton took nothing from me. In fact, he refused saying, "You're a good woman and a very genuine woman. I am sorry for what has happened to you in my country. I feel ashamed. It is bad luck on Boaz's part that he didn't see the love you had for him."

"Well, I think Boaz loved my money more than he did me."

I told him I had a few things still at the house he might be interested in and to come round. He later bought my precious stereo and I gave him my chest of drawers as a thank you. There was a nice, pale blue shirt I'd brought back from America for Boaz, which you didn't have to iron. Boaz called it his '*Wash and Go*' shirt.

"If you don't mind I would like you to have it. He only wore it a few times and it's clean." It would suit you. He was happy to accept.

Everything I bought was brand new and now I'm selling if for next to nothing. But it all had to go, except for one thing; the mirror Boaz had made for me. As usual he had left me in the house all day on my own. When he arrived back I was just about to ask him where he'd been, when this man appeared behind him and started bringing something in. Boaz told him to put whatever it was in the bedroom. Boaz never said anything else but when the guy left I went into the bedroom and there it was. The most beautiful, wooden handcrafted mirror. It had a drawer at the bottom and carved into the wood was a huge love heart. I'd told Boaz I couldn't find a nice mirror. Of course, now I felt guilty for fighting with him. That was Boaz; he had the knack of pissing you off and then doing something from the heart.

I did think about staying in Uganda as I really do like the country; the weather, the nature and the people are really nice and there's no language barrier. It's just unfortunate that what happened to me makes me wary to stay. One of Robert's clients was a renowned builder and he'd shown an interest in employing me as a Supervisor on one of his projects. I met up with him and he was a nice old guy; quite a character. But the job never happened. I kept calling him but he never answered the phone. I couldn't be bothered with this. I was sick to death of chasing people. I think I might have stayed in Uganda if the job had materialized. Now there was nothing to keep me here.

It was August 2014 when I booked my ticket to London, which cost £500 and started packing up. It had taken less than three months to have all my money taken from me. It took another six months for a court to take on my case. And it had taken another year, after Boaz's death, to tie everything up and gather together enough money to leave. To say I'd been trapped in this country was an understatement. I did what I had to do, not what I set out to do.

I finally found a decent shipping company. I was still counting every last penny. In the end it cost me $1,000 US dollars to ship back six boxes. All I had in the world were now in six cardboard boxes, sitting in the corner of my living room. A lot less than the load I'd originally shipped over. But I wanted to keep the costs down. And I didn't want to drag a load of stuff home especially as I wasn't sure where I'd be living. A friend called Cheryl, who lived in Essex, had offered me a room until I got sorted. But I didn't think I wanted to return to England straightaway. I decided to have a stopover in Cairo, Egypt. I just wanted to rest; lie in the sun and forget about everything.

I spent my last night at Charlotte's house and had a few farewell drinks. I didn't say a proper goodbye to anyone but left a few gifts with Charlotte to give to the people I had met down Nabe Road. The people, who helped me, supported me and had become my friends.

The taxi arrived and Charlotte came with me to the airport. As we drove away, Peter ran after the car. "Goodbye Madam, good luck Madam." I gave Peter a few gifts before I left. He was always so grateful over the smallest of things, even a fried egg sandwich. I gave him a nice pair of *Nike* leather trainers and my *Merrell* shoes and some combat trousers; we were about the same size so it was his lucky day. I felt sad and wasn't happy to leave but it was the right thing to do. But I was apprehensive about my future. After paying for everything, I had hardly any money left. And England was a lot more expensive than Uganda. And a hell of a lot colder.

Arriving at the airport we said our goodbyes. It was an emotional farewell for me and Charlotte. We had become really good friends and I will miss her. It was such a relief to get through passport control. I just wanted to get on the plane.

As we took off I was in tears looking out the window. The beautiful scenery of Uganda was disappearing out of sight and the chance of love and happiness had died along with Boaz. This enormous feeling of guilt took hold of me. Someone had died because of me. In just over two years my life had been turned upside down. I'd gone from being in love to losing everything. I was still struggling to come to terms with the fact Boaz was dead.

They say there are five stages of grief: denial, anger, bargaining, depression and acceptance. It's possible that I'm grieving over somebody that never existed or never really loved me. So I skipped the first four stages of grieving and moved straight to the depression.

I had booked five nights in a hotel in Giza not far from Cairo and close to the Pyramids. I had always wanted to see the Pyramids. It would help me to forget and open my eyes to something new. It was a three-and-a-half-hour flight from Uganda to Egypt and when I landed it was very busy and disorganized. I found myself a taxi and made my way to the hotel. There'd recently been some terrorist activity so everywhere was quiet. But that didn't bother me; less tourists, easier to get around.

But it was hard to switch off. I kept thinking of the significance of the date 6th August and the strange events surrounding and leading up to Boaz's death. But I do know it's a date I will never forget. The day Boaz asked me to marry him was 6th August 2011. Then, he called me out of the blue on 6th August 2013. And not long after that phone call he was dead. Ironically, after all the silence between us, I was probably the last person he spoke to. My friend Robert thought Boaz was saying goodbye to me. Yet another unanswered question I will never find the answer to.

I don't think he was a bad person however; in the end he was extremely good at being bad. He managed to rip me to pieces both physically and mentally. No, I think he was tempted by all that money. I'm sure we are all guilty of that; I call it *The Devil's Paper*. Why call it that? Because money is the root of all evil; we fight over it, want more of it, divorce over it. There is never enough and it brings us so much pain when in the wrong hands. Money turned even Boaz from the sweet guy I fell for into a Devil. Sadly, it seems we cannot live without this horrible thing called money. He held on tight to the money until money controlled him and that's when his troubles began. It seems my weakness was falling in love. It made me vulnerable; vulnerable to those who wanted to exploit it.

I organized a driver to take me to the Pyramids and was surprised how built-up the area was around them. You turn a street corner, go behind some shops, through a barrier and there they are. Wow, they took my breath away. I spent around four hours with a guide taking pictures. Then I found a nice restaurant to finish off the day before heading back to the hotel. I was determined to have a good time and swallowed every lump in my throat in an effort to hold back the tears.

The next day I took a taxi to a major souk in the Islamic district of Cairo and then went on to the Egyptian Museum. I spent the rest of the time by the pool, sleeping, crying and thinking. I thought about what Judge Kabiito had said; that my story would make a good book. Maybe that's what I was destined to do; maybe it will help me get through the tragedy. After all, I don't want Boaz's death to be for nothing. Maybe he died so I could live to tell our story.

Spiritually I could feel Boaz everywhere; following me. It was as if he was hanging on, trying to make things right. Of course he wasn't ready to die. He was so young and still had a lot of unfinished business to sort out, especially with me. When I saw him he was lying in the mortuary. When I heard him he was crying, wanting to come back into the world of the living and when I felt him, it was the warmth of his hand on my face.

 Now, as I heard, 'Welcome to London Heathrow,' I had a plan. I will write that book like the Judge suggested. The story of a boy called Boaz and how he stole my heart. Maybe I will send a copy to Judge Kabiito and tell him about my 'great escape.' And pass on my thanks, of course.

Boaz will always remain a mystery to me, along with his death and even death itself. But the mystery continues and has left me open-minded to the stories of old. I recently learnt that a week after Boaz died, his Grandmother passed away; her name was Ruth.

I want to thank my friends from the USA from the UK and Uganda, that help me supported me and believed in me when I asked for help they guided me, without judgement or questioning. Without their help I would not be alive today I would not be able to tell my story.

Randy and Cathee Cornelison
William Huckins
Sean Waller
Scott Veitch
Enoch Machelikim
Charlotte Kemigisha
Robert Irumba
Gary & Viola Denton
Muwanga Joshua
Kwesiga Rwampororo
Cecilia Lwanga
Judge Justice Kabiito
Ochen Kelly
Nalweyiso Jackline
Julius Kaziro
Mbidde Eria
Elizabeth Sanyu Namala
Betty
Bwende Peter
Kenny Steel

I might be the survivor but you are the heroes. I am forever grateful.

Lightning Source UK Ltd.
Milton Keynes UK
UKOW05n2313300617

304454UK00005B/29/P

9 781526 202567